THE EVERYTHING®
Practice Interview Book

Dear Reader,

Interviews are difficult. I know—I've been on both sides of the desk. I've interviewed job candidates and I've been interviewed. Honestly I can think of many things that are more fun. Of course, there's a lot of pressure on the job candidate. You can attest to that. You want to let the interviewer know you are the best candidate for the job. But there's also a lot of pressure on the interviewer, who wants to make sure the person she hires is a good fit for the job and for the company in general.

In the six years I've been managing the Career Planning site on About.com (*http://careerplanning.about.com*), I've often heard from people who are stressed out over the job interview. Most people want to know what questions to expect and how to answer them. I get a lot of e-mail from people who have faced improper or illegal questions on an interview. I made a point of including a lot of information on that topic.

I wrote this book with all that in mind. Over 300 interview questions help prepare you for anything you might face. Read the answers carefully and use them to guide you in putting together your own responses.

Good Luck!

Dawn Rosenberg McKay

The EVERYTHING Series

Editorial

Publishing Director	Gary M. Krebs
Managing Editor	Kate McBride
Copy Chief	Laura MacLaughlin
Acquisitions Editors	Bethany Brown / Kate Burgo
Development Editor	Christina MacDonald
Production Editors	Jamie Wielgus
	Bridget Brace

Production

Production Director	Susan Beale
Production Manager	Michelle Roy Kelly
Series Designers	Daria Perreault
	Colleen Cunningham
Cover Design	Paul Beatrice
	Frank Rivera
Layout and Graphics	Colleen Cunningham
	Rachael Eiben
	Michelle Roy Kelly
	John Paulhus
	Daria Perreault
	Erin Ring
Series Cover Artist	Barry Littmann

THE
EVERYTHING®
PRACTICE
INTERVIEW
BOOK

Be prepared for any question

Dawn Rosenberg McKay

Adams Media
Avon, Massachusetts

To Dean and Rebecca for their patience.

An Everything® Series Book.
Everything® and everything.com® are registered trademarks of F+W Publications, Inc.

Published by Adams Media, an F+W Publications Company
57 Littlefield Street, Avon, MA 02322 U.S.A.
www.adamsmedia.com

ISBN 13: 978-1-59337-133-3
ISBN 10: 1-59337-133-0
Printed in Canada.

J I H G F

Library of Congress Cataloging-in-Publication Data
McKay, Dawn Rosenberg.
The everything practice interview book / Dawn Rosenberg McKay.
      p.   cm.
ISBN 1-59337-133-0
1. Employment interviewing. I. Title. II. Series: Everything series.
HF5549.5.I6M327 2004
650.14'4–dc22

                                    2004005401

This book is available at quantity discounts for bulk purchases.
For information, call 1-800-289-0963

Contents

Top Ten Things
Not to Say on a Job Interview

1. That suit looks expensive! How much money do you make, anyway?

2. What would my salary be? I have to make more than I did at my last job.

3. I've never heard of your company before. What type of business is this?

4. It wasn't my fault. My coworkers had it in for me.

5. My boss was a jerk. I didn't have to think twice about quitting after what he did.

6. How much time do you give for maternity leave?

7. How many vacation days will I have each year? I love to travel. I was thinking of Australia next year.

8. If someone files a harassment charge against me, you would cover for me, right?

9. I'd rather be working in my own field, but I can't find anyone who will hire me, so this will do for now.

10. Can I have my own office? I really don't like working with other people.

Introduction

WOULDN'T IT BE NICE IF YOU COULD send out your resume for a position you're qualified for and simply be offered a job? After all, everything about you is right there on your resume, isn't it? You should know—you put it there yourself.

But, no, everything about you is not on your resume. Think of your resume as a pencil drawing of who you really are. There is no dimension to it. It has no color and no expression. Basically, it's pretty flat. Not at all like you; you are multifaceted. You've made choices throughout your career. You reached certain goals and had many accomplishments. You should have a chance to talk about all of that, because those details are what will make an employer want to hire you.

The job interview is your chance to show your prospective employer who you really are and what you can bring to the position. By asking you questions, a prospective employer can learn all about you and why you made the choices you made. He can discover what motivates you and what makes you proud. The interviewer can find out how you will fit in with his company. Will you get along with other employees? Will you make important contributions to his organization?

There is a lot to accomplish during the job interview. It is perhaps the most important part of the entire job search process. It is also the most difficult part of the entire job search process. It's not like the resume you spent months poring over. You can edit your resume again and again until it lists the most important things about your career, using the most effective wording to highlight your skills. However, a job interview usually takes place in under an hour. When you say something, there's no delete key. If you forget to say something, the moment may have already passed by the time you realize it. You can't just insert it.

That is why it is so very important that you prepare well for the job interview. You won't have another chance to get it right, at least not with the same employer. The more comfortable you are with the entire process of interviewing, the more relaxed you will be when it comes time for the interview, and the better the interview will be.

This book will guide you through the entire job interview process. The first two chapters cover everything you need to do before the interview takes place. Discover what you need to do to prepare for a job interview. Learn how to research a prospective employer so you can intelligently ask and answer questions during your interview. Find out how to dress for an interview. Learn about interviewing in another country.

Next up are twelve chapters that are packed full of sample job interview questions. For each question there is a great answer, an explanation of why you should give that answer, and then an answer you should never give and the reason why. As you go through the questions, think of how you would personalize each answer.

The final chapter deals with the aftermath of the job interview. Find out what you need to do to follow up on a job interview. Is a thank-you letter really necessary? Of course, the whole purpose of this entire process is to get a job offer. Find out how to negotiate, accept, or reject one. By the time you're finished with this book, you'll be able to take on even the toughest interview.

CHAPTER 1

Preparing for the Interview

MANY PEOPLE FOLLOW A CERTAIN ROUTINE when they are job hunting. They send copies of their resumes to prospective employers and follow that with weeks of sitting around waiting to be called back. You should let your competition follow that routine—you can make much better use of your time! By preparing for a job interview in advance, you will increase your chances of getting hired when you finally do get that call.

Understanding Job Interviews

Before you begin interviewing, you must make sure you have a good understanding of what interviews are all about. You should know about the interview process, what the different types of interviews are, and what employers are trying to learn about you from an interview. Becoming more knowledgeable about what to expect will help you demystify the entire interview process. This in turn will allow you to feel more confident when you are on a job interview. Remember, the more confident you feel, the more confident you will look to your potential boss.

The Purpose of the Interview

Have you ever wondered what the point of a job interview even is? The employer has your resume—can't she just look at it to see whether you have the necessary skills and experience? All she should need to do is make a phone call or two to verify that information, right? While it is made up of information about your past experience, your resume doesn't give the employer a full picture of who you are. Your resume is only a summary of your skills, work experience, and educational background. With only your resume to rely on, the person interviewing you won't have any idea of the specific things about you that will set you apart from the other candidates.

After all, a resume is merely a piece of paper and you are so much more than that. An interviewer can't learn about someone's personality by looking at a resume. She can't discover how a candidate developed some of his skills or which accomplishments meant the most to him. The interviewer can't find out how the candidate reacts to change or adversity by reading his resume.

The only way an interviewer can learn any of those things about a job candidate is by talking to him and asking questions. This will allow the candidate to paint a picture of himself that is much more elaborate than what can fit on one sheet of paper.

 ESSENTIAL

Remember that the interview is your chance to embellish the facts you listed on your resume. Rather than looking at an interview as an inquisition, you should instead look at it as a wonderful opportunity to express your true self to your prospective employer.

Another purpose of a job interview is to help you to learn about the employer. You will discover things on a job interview that will allow you to make an informed decision about whether to accept or reject an offer, should the employer make one. You will learn some things about the employer by asking questions. You will also learn things about the employer from the questions she asks you. For example, if the interviewer starts asking questions about working late or traveling, you can safely assume that these things will be part of your life should you be hired.

You may decide by the end of a job interview that this isn't really the job for you or that this company isn't one you want to work for. And that's okay. It is in everyone's best interests, both the employer's and yours, to make this determination before you accept a job offer and begin working.

 ALERT!

If you decide at the end of a job interview that you don't want to work for the employer, don't say anything just yet. Wait twenty-four hours before you let the employer know of your decision. After thinking it over, you may change your mind.

The Interview Process

The interview process can go on for quite a while. First, you may be asked to come in for a screening interview. The screening interview is your first interview with a particular employer. In some cases it may even take place over the telephone. During a screening interview, the person interviewing you (usually someone who works in the human resources department) will want to verify items that are on your resume, such as dates of employment, schooling, etc.

If the person who completes your screening interview is satisfied, he will most likely set up a selection interview. While someone from human resources may interview you again at this point, it is also likely that a department manager will interview you. The department manager, in addition to making sure you have the desirable skills and background, will want to make sure you have the right personality for the position.

Following the first selection interview, the employer may ask you to come back for subsequent interviews. During these further interviews, the employer may want to introduce you to other people in the company to make sure you are the right choice. Remember, you are still in the interviewing phase, so be on your best behavior.

The employer may call back other candidates as well, as she tries to narrow down her choices. Sometimes you will be the only candidate who is asked to return for more interviews. That usually is good news, but don't consider it a done deal until you actually have a job offer.

 QUESTION?

What should I discuss on a second interview?
Use this opportunity to bring up something that you didn't get to talk about during the initial interview. Be prepared with an example of a specific skill or achievement you didn't have a chance to highlight before. Remember to explain how the example shows that you are a good candidate for the particular position you want.

Preparing to Answer Questions

You will be asked a variety of questions on a job interview. These questions will pertain to your skills and abilities, accomplishments, education, and work history. You will also be asked questions about your strengths and weaknesses, your interests and hobbies, and your likes and dislikes, all of which will allow the employer to learn about your personal traits or characteristics.

In Chapters 3 through 13 you will find questions you might encounter on a job interview. While answers (both good and bad) are given, they are only a guideline. You should try to figure out how *you* will answer those questions. While you should not go into a job interview with a memorized script, you should have an idea of how you will answer most questions that will come your way. Chapter 14 will give you ideas for the types of questions you should ask the interviewer. Use these questions in the same way—as a guideline to be adapted to your particular situation and the company and industry you are interviewing with.

Special Types of Interviews

At some point during your job search, you may find that you have to participate in a group interview. This means several candidates will be interviewed at one time. A group interview allows those who are natural leaders to show themselves, and often the purpose of this type of interview is to find out who stands out from the crowd or emerges as a leader. If you aren't a leader, don't worry—not everyone can be. The job may simply not be the right one for you. Trying to be someone you're not will only make things difficult down the line, when you or your employer discover that you're not the right fit after all.

If you walk into an interview and find yourself sitting at a table opposite several people, don't be alarmed. You are about to take part in a panel interview. This type of interview is also known as a committee interview and is often used when a group of people must collectively decide who to hire. During a panel interview, each member of the panel will ask you questions. The best thing you can do in this situation is stay calm and take the questions one at a time.

 ESSENTIAL

During a panel interview, several people may be firing questions off at once. Listen carefully, but if you don't hear the question, politely ask the person who asked it to repeat herself. When answering questions during a panel interview, directly address the person who asked the question by making eye contact with her.

Learning about Yourself

Your goal on a job interview is to give the best answers you can possibly give. In order to do that there's someone you need to get to know—yourself. You probably worked hard at putting together a great resume that highlights your skills, accomplishments, and experience. This was time well spent, since a great resume will help you line up the right interview, but there is only so much that will come across in a resume. You need to uncover what is behind that basic outline so you can present it to the interviewer and show him what an excellent candidate you really are.

Be Specific

On a job interview you will be asked questions about your skills, for example. Of course, you know what skills you have, but can you discuss how you acquired them? What if you're asked about your accomplishments? You've no doubt accomplished a lot at work, but can you recall specifics? You need anecdotes that clearly back up your claims, so it is imperative that you think back in advance and have some good examples of your strengths ready when the subject comes up.

Go Beyond the Resume

The interviewer will likely use your resume to guide him through the interview. You should be intimately familiar with each item you have listed on it. Study your resume before you go out on an interview. You must be prepared to talk about and elaborate on everything that is on it.

 FACT

Interviewers generally expect more than yes or no answers to their questions. You must give details that clearly explain your answer. When an interviewer asks you to discuss a particular situation, be ready to give examples.

Sit down with a clean copy of your resume and a notebook in front of you. Now, one at a time, look at each job you have listed on your resume and think about it carefully. What do you remember about the job? Do you remember why you started working there and why you left? What was it like working there? Take notes so you can study them later.

You should try to recall details about the job beyond what you put on your resume. Did your boss rely on you to perform certain duties because of a particular strength you possess? Can you recall times when you were invaluable to your employer?

Do you remember which job was your favorite (or least favorite)? Can you recall what you liked (or disliked) about each one? Think about some projects you worked on. What skills did you use in order to complete those projects? What obstacles did you have to overcome to complete them? Did you most often work on a team or alone? Can you give examples of projects you worked on as part of a team and those you worked on independently?

 ALERT!

Don't exaggerate on your resume. Hopefully it won't be too late for you to heed this warning, but if it is, please remember it for next time. If the information on your resume isn't completely true, you will find that it is impossible to discuss it during a job interview without continuing to exaggerate or lie. By the time you are done, if you have not been caught, you will have presented yourself as a totally different person than who you really are.

A solid resume will list your major accomplishments. Try to remember what you put into achieving each one. Did the accomplishment help you reach a goal? How did it benefit the employer? Were you in any way rewarded for your achievement, perhaps with a promotion? If you take the time to recall all this information before your interview, you don't have to worry about long silences as you try to remember the facts while the pressure's on.

Learning about Your Prospective Employer

It is important that you learn as much as possible about a prospective employer before you walk into a job interview. Your knowledge will allow you to intelligently answer questions you may be asked, and ask a few of your own. You can also use what you learn to help you make an informed decision about whether or not to accept a job should the employer offer you one. Gathering information about a prospective employer will require some effort on your part, but it is in your best interests to do so.

Public versus Private Companies

Before you begin your research, you should first figure out whether your prospective employer is a publicly held company or a privately held company. Publicly held companies are those with shareholders who have a financial stake in the company. Privately held companies are owned by individuals or groups of individuals.

Publicly held companies generally are required to disclose information about finances quarterly and information about material events or corporate changes as they occur, so you may have an easier time finding information if the company you are researching is public.

There are several ways to find out if the company you are researching is publicly held. On the Internet, visit the Securities and Exchange Commission Web site at *www.sec.gov* and search for the company by name. Print resources include the *Directory of Companies Required to File Annual Reports with the Securities and Exchange Commission Under the Securities Exchange Act of 1934*, published by the Securities and Exchange Commission, and the *Annual Guide to Stocks*. Both are available in many public and academic libraries.

All sorts of information about publicly held companies can be found in the reports they must file with the United States Securities and Exchange Commission. You can download these files from the Securities and Exchange Commission's Web site.

You can also obtain a copy of a company's annual reports directly from the company, usually by calling its shareholder relations department.

 FACT

Not all publicly held companies have to file annual and periodic reports with the U.S. Securities and Exchange Commission. Only companies that have over $10 million in assets and securities held by more than 500 owners must file these reports.

While it has traditionally been more difficult to find information about privately held companies, it is not as difficult to obtain this information as it once was. Thanks to the advent of the World Wide Web, a lot of information that wasn't available to the public before is now available. (Keep reading for more hints on Internet research.)

What You Should Know

There is basic information you should know about an employer. Obviously you should know what a prospective employer's line of business is. You should know what products or services they sell. You should know who their customers or clients are. If the job you are interested in involves direct client contact, it's even more important for you to know about those clients.

The more information you have about a prospective employer, the better. In addition to knowing basic information like the employer's line of business, you should also try to obtain financial information. A company's financial condition should play an important role in helping you determine whether or not you should accept a job offer. It may not be a good idea to accept a job offer from a company that is in poor financial health. Who knows how long that job will be around once you take it?

You should also know something about a company's history.

Find out what year the company was founded and who founded it. Learn what the company's mission was and is. Has the company changed its focus over the years? Find out if the company ever faced any difficulties and how it overcame those difficulties.

 ESSENTIAL

If you have been away from your career for an extended period of time, it is especially important that you keep up with any developments and changes in the field. A leave of absence from the work force isn't an excuse to ignore current events.

Staying on top of the latest news about your prospective employer, the industry, and your profession is also imperative. Find out if there are any changes such as mergers or acquisitions on the horizon and what effect these changes will have on the company and its employees. You should learn whether the company has released any new products lately and how the public has reacted to these new products. You should be aware of any changes that are occurring in the industry and in your profession as well.

You should also have details about the job in question. If you don't have a job announcement, check the employer's Web site to see if you can find one there. It is perfectly appropriate for you to ask for a detailed job description when the employer calls to invite you to come in for an interview. The more you know about the job, the better you will be able to demonstrate to the employer that you are the best person to fill it.

Doing Your Research

So how do you find all of this information? Don't panic, you're in luck. It's never been easier to do company research than it is right now. Before the birth of the World Wide Web, if you wanted to do research you had to go to the library. Even then, you could look through massive business directories and only come up with tiny bits of information about a company. Now, having a computer with an Internet connection allows you to do your research from home at any time. But don't stop there—there are other useful resources you should be aware of.

Internet Researching

Many companies use Web sites to tell the public about themselves. A corporate Web site is a great place to get basic information about privately held as well as publicly held companies. You can learn about a company's products and services, key personnel, and even employment opportunities. Companies will often announce news on their Web sites.

Use a search engine to search for a company's name. Because the cost of putting up a Web site is relatively low, companies of all sizes have one. Your search results page will probably include the company's Web site as well as links to other Web pages that reference the company.

 FACT

Do you want to figure out which Web site on your results list belongs to the company? Look at the URLs listed there—the company's URL will often include the company's name. For example, the URL for Adams Media, the publisher of this book, is ✑*www.adamsmedia.com.*

The company's main Web site will probably be of most help to you, but don't ignore all other pages that mention the company. While you have the results list in front of you, take a look at some of them—they may contain pertinent information about your prospective employer.

Newspapers and Journals

If you want to keep up with company or industry news on a regular basis, you should read the business section of your city's newspaper. For information on larger companies, read the *Wall Street Journal* or the business section of the *New York Times*.

You can access the *New York Times* online. Articles from the last seven days are free but you will have to pay a small fee if you want to see articles that are older than that. If you want to read the *Wall Street Journal* online you must pay for a subscription.

Regional business journals or newspapers are another good source for company news, especially for smaller local companies. NewsLink is a Web site that lists those publications along with a link to each one's Web site. You can find NewsLink at *www.newslink.org*.

Proprietary Resources

In addition to what you will find on the World Wide Web, company information can often be found in proprietary, or subscription-based, resources. Proprietary resources are those that can be accessed only by those who pay a subscription fee.

 ESSENTIAL

The subscription fee for proprietary resources is usually quite hefty, so generally subscribers are institutional entities. Check with your library to find out what online resources they subscribe to. You may even be able to access some of these resources from home.

Proprietary resources include databases that index articles from various publications. Sometimes these articles appear in full text and can be downloaded and printed out. Sometimes you will see only the title of the article or a short extract and have to figure out where you can get the article you want. You may be able to purchase it from the database publisher or from the publication that originally ran the article. You may also be able to request the article from your local library. If they don't have it, they may be able to retrieve it from another library through interlibrary loan.

Company Directories

Company directories will give you descriptive information about many different companies. These resources can give you an unbiased look at your prospective employer, which for obvious reasons the company's own Web site or brochures will not.

Many company directories are proprietary. Subscription-only directories contain more extensive information than those that are free. Many include a company profile, financial data, and links to articles that have been written about the company.

One directory is Hoovers Online, which can be found at *www.hoovers.com*. This directory has some areas that can be accessed at no charge and others that are available by subscription only. Once on this site, you can search for a company by name or by stock ticker symbol. If the company you're looking for is in the database, you will be able to access a fact sheet about the company. These basic fact sheets are free, but areas that offer more in-depth information are proprietary and you will need to purchase a subscription to access them.

Ⓔ ALERT!

If you learned something about your prospective employer that puts the company in a bad light, think carefully before you bring it up. It may be a sensitive topic for the person interviewing you.

Take Time to Rehearse

In preparing for job interviews it is important that you do some practice interviewing, both alone and with others. Rehearsing for interviews will allow you to work on any problems that may be viewed as negatives by the interviewer. Rehearsing will also allow you to become more comfortable with the interview process. By the time you go on an interview, you will have no problem confidently answering questions.

The interview is not only about what you say, but also about how you say it. It is difficult to see yourself as you appear to others. When engaged in conversation with someone, do you tend to look disinterested or do you generally look engaged? Do you look nervous or calm? Do you talk too fast, too slowly, too softly, or too loudly? You probably don't know the answers unless someone has pointed out a problem to you in the past.

To get a glimpse of what you look like when having a conversation with someone, you might want to begin rehearsing for your job interview in front of a mirror. When doing this, study your body language. Are your hands clasped tightly in your lap? Are your arms folded across your chest? Are you smiling? Remember your body language speaks volumes, so take a look at Chapter 2 to find out what is appropriate and what to avoid.

 FACT

> Toastmasters International is a nonprofit organization dedicated to helping people strengthen their communication skills. Members receive help in areas such as organization, voice inflection, and persuasiveness. There are over 9,300 Toastmasters clubs located around the world. You can find one near you by going to ✎*www.toastmasters.org.*

Next, you should recruit a friend to help you rehearse. If you know someone who has experience interviewing others, especially someone who is responsible for hiring, try to get that person to work with you. If not, find someone else whose opinion you trust. Have that person ask you questions and answer them as if you were on an actual interview. To make the situation more realistic, have your friend choose the questions to ask.

If you have several friends who are job hunting, you can all practice interviewing together. Videotape yourselves interviewing one another and then play back the tapes. Critique one another's performances as well as your own. Once you get through that, the real thing will seem so much easier.

Access Your Network

A network is a group of individuals you can to turn for help. Your network may consist of people you've worked with in the past, your friends, and relatives. Not only is it possible that these people can help you, but they have networks of their own and may know someone else who can give you advice. Eventually, if you branch out far enough, you're bound to find someone who knows something about one of the companies you're interested in.

Most people think of their networks only when they are trying to find out about employment opportunities. However, a great time to access your network is when you have been asked to come in for a job interview. There may be members of your network who previously worked for the company you are interviewing with or who know someone who has worked there or currently works there. Someone in your network may have interviewed there in the past or may know the person who is interviewing you.

 ALERT!

Be cautious about revealing anything you learned through your network. If you start talking about something that wasn't released to the public, the interviewer will want to know how you got your information.

Imagine all the valuable information you can get from someone who has had some sort of contact with the company you are interviewing with. You can learn things you would not be able to learn anywhere else. Sure, there are resources you can use to learn about a company's finances or to find up-to-date news, as discussed earlier. Someone on your network, though, may be able to tell you that the person who is interviewing you will be very impressed by the fact that you speak four languages and will tell you not to wear anything green because the interviewer really hates it.

Dealing with Anxiety

For some people, preparing for a job interview just doesn't do the trick when it comes to alleviating anxiety. You may have dealt with your fear of the unknown by learning all you can about job interviews. You may know what questions to anticipate and how you will answer them. You may have rehearsed for the interview. Still, you can't get rid of the butterflies that are fluttering around in your stomach.

If you've done everything you can to prepare, as discussed earlier, you have tremendously increased your chances for succeeding on an interview. You should be able to walk into the interview calm, cool, and collected, and bursting with confidence. However, if you aren't relaxed, you won't be able to do that. Don't let your anxiety take away from your performance on a job interview. Find a way to relieve your stress before it affects your chances of getting the job you want.

 FACT

When people are asked to rank life events in order of the amount of stress felt when dealing with that event, they rank a change in employment high up on that list. With that in mind, it's perfectly normal to be anxious about a job interview.

There are many techniques people use to relieve stress. You should know which techniques work well for you and utilize them in the days leading up to your job interview.

Many people swear by exercise as a great way to relieve anxiety. If exercise is one of the ways you de-stress, an early morning run before an interview or a workout at the gym may help you.

If strenuous exercise isn't something you are used to, it may not be wise to start a new exercise regimen the day of your interview. Perhaps you should take a tension-relieving walk in the park or around town instead. Other techniques you can try are massage therapy, meditation, or deep-breathing exercises.

What to Do about Low Confidence

Sometimes job searches can take a very long time. This is especially true during economic downturns. People are sometimes out of work for months or even a year at a time. This can be very rough on a person's ego. If you are in this situation, your confidence may wane and you may doubt whether you will ever find a job.

Your lack of confidence will be very visible to anyone you come into contact with. That includes prospective employers. You must get out of your slump and do it fast, or you won't be hired—not because of a bad economy, but because of the way you carry yourself.

 ALERT!

Do whatever it takes to boost your confidence, because a lack of it will sabotage your chances of getting hired. If you are nervous during a job interview, you won't look confident and will be too distracted to answer questions to the best of your ability. If you are anxious in the days leading up to an interview, you will lose sleep and won't be well rested.

Earlier, you were advised to look at your resume to learn more about yourself. Now would be a good time to zoom in on your accomplishments. Remember all the great things you did in your career. Think about what you can bring to a new job. Think about how lucky any employer would be to have you work for her. Focus on these things, and the interviewer will notice them too.

The Night Before and Morning of the Interview

Spend a relaxing evening at home the night before an interview. Soaking in a hot tub and curling up with a good book is sure to calm you down. If you can, try not to think about the job interview. Have some caffeine-free herbal tea to help you relax. Remember, caffeine can be found in substances other than coffee, including chocolate. It can also be found in many over-the-counter medications. Read labels carefully and when in doubt, avoid taking anything that may act as a stimulant and keep you from getting a good night's sleep.

Get to bed early if possible. You will want to have a full night's sleep so you appear well rested for the interview. Dark circles under the eyes never enhanced anyone's looks. If you are sleepy, you won't be alert and therefore may have difficulty paying attention during the interview.

Give yourself plenty of time in the morning to get ready. If you have to rush around, you will only add to your anxiety. Be ready to deal with any problems you didn't anticipate, like a run in your stockings or a stain on your favorite shirt. Make sure you have backups.

Don't forget to eat a good breakfast before you leave the house. Nutritionists have told us for years that this is the best way to start off your day right. If you are hungry, you won't be able to concentrate. Besides, a growling stomach during a job interview would be very embarrassing.

Don't overdo your coffee consumption the day of your interview. Many people get jittery from even just a little too much caffeine. Of course, the day of your interview is not the time to go cold turkey. You should have a cup of coffee if you need it to get you going, but don't have two, three, or four cups. If you are already feeling a little nervous, this will just exacerbate it.

CHAPTER 2

First Impressions Count

YOU HAVE WORKED HARD RESEARCHING your prospective employer and you know what you need to say to convince him that you are the best candidate for the job. But wait, there's one more thing to think about before the big day—the first impression. Your physical appearance, what you do when you meet the interviewer, and your body language during the interview all contribute to the opinion your interviewer will form of you. Be prepared to make a great first impression even before you open your mouth.

What to Wear to the Interview

Most people are troubled by the thought of what to wear for a job interview. They wonder if they should wear casual clothes or formal attire. They question whether to choose bright colors or neutral tones. Even among fashionistas, there is quite a bit of disagreement over what is appropriate to wear for a job interview.

Some experts feel that regardless of the culture of the company, a person should always wear a suit for an interview. Other experts feel that wearing a suit is not necessary in some situations, and worse, could even be inappropriate. Are you even more confused now? Don't be. Here are some pointers to help you decide on an outfit that will help you shine on a job interview.

When Should You Wear a Suit?

If you are interviewing for a job in a traditionally conservative field, such as accounting, finance, or law, the answer to the question "What should I wear?" is a simple one. Both men and women must wear suits. You should choose a conservative color, like black, gray, or navy blue.

It is best to own at least two suits. If you buy two, you won't have to worry about what to do when you get called back for a second interview. You will also be a step ahead when you get a job offer and those suits become a regular part of your wardrobe. Buy a conservative rather than a trendy suit and always buy the best quality you can afford. You can wear the same suit for several years if you stick to these rules.

 FACT

If you want to get the best prices on business attire, remember that men's suits are often on sale during April and November. Men's shirts go on sale in January and July, and the best months to buy shoes are January, July, November, and December.

Underneath the suit, you should wear a solid, preferably white or light-colored shirt or blouse. A man should wear a necktie. A woman can accessorize with a silk scarf, if she wishes. Both ties and scarves should have simple designs and not be brightly colored. Women's scarves should be short or of medium length since a long scarf could get in the way.

Is Casual Dress Ever Appropriate?

As you can see, your choices of what to wear are limited when you are interviewing in a conservative field. That is not necessarily a bad thing—at least it makes your decision easy. Just ask anyone who is interviewing for a job in a field where the mode of dress is not so clearly defined. The definition of proper interview attire in a casual office is something not all experts agree on, whether you ask those who work in fashion or those who work in career planning.

While some feel that a formal suit is appropriate for all job interviews, others, this author included, feel that what you wear on an interview should ideally be similar to what you will wear on the job should you be hired. When you have a job interview, you want the interviewer to envision you as a member of her staff. The way you dress can help her do that.

Of course, a job interview should be considered a "special occasion" and not just a typical day at the office. Therefore, your attire should be a notch or two above what you would wear to work. If, for example, typical dress in the workplace you're interested in joining is "casual," you should opt for dress pants and a coordinating sport jacket for men, and dress pants, a skirt, or a dress and coordinated blazer for women.

A company's corporate culture usually dictates how employees dress. You can try to learn more about a prospective employer's corporate culture from the research you do in preparation for the job interview. Usually companies in more creative industries have less stringent dress codes.

 ESSENTIAL

If you can't find a company's dress code standards through traditional research, hanging out near the building's entrance at the beginning of a work day will allow you to see what people look like when they arrive for work. Avoid doing this on a Friday, as that is the day of the week many companies allow "casual dress" regardless of what they allow on other days.

If you have exhausted all ways of finding out how employees of the company dress, you might have to wear a suit. If given the choice between overdressing for a job interview or underdressing for one, you are better off being overdressed. In other words, it is more acceptable to be the only job candidate who shows up in a suit rather than the only one who does not.

The Finer Details

More important than what you wear to a job interview is how you wear it. Check your clothing to make sure it is stain-free. Also make sure it is free of wrinkles. The last thing you want is to look like you rolled out of the hamper. It is worth bringing your suit to the dry cleaner to have it professionally cleaned and pressed.

Women should stay away from low-cut necklines or skirts with short hemlines. Revealing outfits may be fine for an evening out after work, but they are not appropriate for the office—any office. Suits should fit properly. That means they should not be too tight or too baggy. If your outfit does not fit you well, a trip to the tailor is in order.

 ALERT!

> Women: Make sure your hosiery is free of runs and visible snags. Carry an extra pair in your purse just in case. Men: Make sure your tie is straight. Invest in a tie tack to keep it in place.

Hair, Makeup, and Nails

Your hair should be neat and clean. The style should be simple. Women's makeup should not be overdone. Lipstick and nail polish should be a neutral color.

Women's nails should be short enough to keep the interviewer from wondering, "How will she get work done with those nails?" Men's nails should be short and clean. Men should be clean-shaven. If you have facial hair, it should be neatly trimmed.

Guidelines for Jewelry

Both men and women should keep jewelry to a bare minimum. That means large dangling earrings, big pendants, and thick chains are out. While body piercings and tattoos may be all the rage in your social circle, remember that some interviewers will be turned off by this. While you are allowed to have your own personal style, a job interview may not be the best place for you to express it. You certainly do not want anything to distract the interviewer from realizing you are the best candidate for the job.

Your Shoes

Finally, it's time to think about your feet, or rather what you are going to put on them. Your shoes are the last thing you will put on before you head off on an interview, but they should not be the last thing you should think about. On the contrary—you should give serious consideration to your footwear.

Conservative colors and styles are the most appropriate shoes to wear on a job interview. Neither men nor women should wear sandals or open-toed shoes of any kind. Black shoes go with everything, even navy blue, according to fashion experts.

Shoes should be in good condition. They do not have to be brand-new, but they should not look like you have hiked miles in them, either. They shouldn't have scuffs on them. If they do, go ahead and polish them.

If you do buy new shoes for interviewing, make sure they are comfortable. It is hard to concentrate on the task at hand when your toes are being pinched. Excessively high heels are out of place on a job interview and in the workplace.

 FACT

One of the first things some job interviewers notice is the condition of a job candidate's shoes. Scuffed, dirty shoes may indicate that the person doesn't pay attention to detail. You can purchase shoe polish and other shoe care supplies at your local drug store.

What to Bring to the Interview

Once you are dressed appropriately, you are ready to walk into the interview with an air of confidence. There are a few things you should always have with you. First and foremost, always bring a few copies of your resume along. The interviewer may want a fresh copy and you may be introduced to other people who will need to see a copy. Put the copies of your resume in a folder to transport them to the interview so they will stay clean and neat.

You may have a portfolio of work samples. If the interviewer has asked to see them or if you think they are noteworthy, bring them with you. Make sure they are neatly compiled and organized. They should represent your best work.

 ESSENTIAL

Arrange your work samples in a binder. The binder should be a conservative color, like black or navy, and should be in good condition. Insert your documents into plastic sheet protectors, available at all office supply stores.

Always carry a pen and a small notebook, in case there is something you want to jot down. Do not forget to bring your date book so you can schedule any future appointments.

You can bring a briefcase with you to carry everything, and women may also carry a small purse. In general, though, you should travel light. Women should not carry large, bulky handbags or anything that looks better suited for a day at the beach. No one should carry a backpack, and shopping bags are definitely out.

Getting to the Interview on Time

There is one thing you can do to sabotage your chances of getting hired even before you shake the interviewer's hand. If you arrive late for the interview, you might as well write your own rejection letter.

Running in at the last minute will throw you off, causing you not to perform as well as you might have had you arrived on time. There are a few things you can do to reduce your risk of being late.

When a prospective employer calls to ask you to come in for an interview, be sure to find out exactly where the interview will take place. Some companies have offices in more than one location. Those locations can be across town or merely across the street from one another. Regardless of the distance between them, you do not want to waste time wandering from one place to another.

Once you know where you have to go, you have to figure out how to get there. If you are driving, map out a route and, if possible, an alternate route just in case you hit some traffic snags along the way. If you have to take a train or a bus, make sure you know which lines you have to ride and which ones you can ride instead if something should happen to interrupt service.

 FACT

If you have access to the Internet, you can plan your trip online. Use mapping Web sites, like *www.mapquest.com*, to plan your trip if you're driving. Many municipal transit systems have their schedules and routes online. You can input your starting point and destination, using landmarks, addresses, or intersections to plan your trip.

You should plan to arrive for your interview early. It is best to get there about ten or fifteen minutes before the time of your appointment. You might want to plan to arrive even earlier than that. If you decide to be an early bird, though, do not show up inside your prospective employer's office any more than ten to fifteen minutes prior to your appointment. Doing so may make the interviewer feel that you are pressuring him to start the interview early.

Arriving for Your Appointment

When you arrive at your prospective employer's offices, you will first announce yourself to the receptionist. Many people do not realize how important this part is. The receptionist is the first employee of the company you will have contact with. As a matter of fact, he or she is the first person every person arriving for an interview meets.

Do not discount the power this person wields. The interviewer may rely on the receptionist to give an opinion of the job candidates. That is one reason it is imperative that you be on your very best behavior right from the start. You might also wind up working with this person. Isn't that why you are there in the first place?

Politely walk up to the reception desk and give the receptionist your name and the name of the person you have an appointment with. You can make small talk about the weather or traffic if you wish. Remember, if you are kept waiting, do not blame the receptionist.

While you are waiting to be called in for the interview, spend your time wisely. You can look over your resume and review any notes you may have prepared. If you finish doing that and still have not been called in, take a look at the professional journals that may be available in the waiting area. Do not read the novel you brought along to read on the train. You want to look like you are busy, not like you are relaxing.

The Interview Begins

Usually the receptionist will announce your arrival and the interviewer will come out to the waiting area to greet you. This is the only chance you will have to make a good first impression. While your behavior during the interview is important, a bad first impression will be very difficult to overcome.

Meeting the Interviewer

When you first meet the interviewer and throughout the interview, you must appear confident, but not smug. You should be assertive, but not aggressive. You should be friendly, but not familiar.

When the interviewer comes out to greet you, the first thing you should do is introduce yourself to him using your first and last name. Do not address him by his first name. Your introduction should sound something like this (feel free to use your own variation): "Hello, Mr. Smith. I'm Joan Brown. It's nice to meet you." You should be ready to shake his hand, but do not offer your hand first. Doing so can put you in an awkward situation if the interviewer does not offer his hand in return. (Handshakes will be discussed later on in the section on body language.)

 FACT

As you proceed to the interviewer's office or to a conference room for the interview, the interviewer may try to make small talk. Stick to things like the weather and stay away from how your favorite team played last night. Your favorite team may turn out to be his team's archrivals, which could result in an awkward moment you don't really need at this point.

Getting Started

Once you arrive in the office where your interview will be held, etiquette dictates that you wait for the interviewer to offer you a seat. However, just because someone is in a position to interview you does not mean he has manners. If the interviewer sits down without first offering you a seat, then sit down across from him or wherever there is an available seat. He is probably in a hurry to get the interview started, so do not waste any time. Get your notebook and pen ready so you will not have to fumble around trying to find them later.

Body Language

When you interact with other people, there are two ways your message gets across to them. One is intentional—your words. The other is often unintentional—your body language. Body language is comprised of the nonverbal gestures and mannerisms that may indicate a person's true feelings.

Your body language can reveal things that your words do not. In fact, it may reveal much more than you intend to reveal. In the simplest terms, if you say you are happy but have a big frown on your face, your body language—the frown—will show your true feelings. While most people manage to exert a great deal of control over the words they let cross their lips, many have great difficulty when it comes to keeping their body language in check.

You may think all this talk about body language is just a bunch of nonsense. However, you must pay attention to what your body language seems to reveal even if you question whether there is any truth to it. Many interviewers are trained to look for even the subtlest nonverbal cues and interpret what they mean. Whether these interpretations are correct is irrelevant as long as the interviewer thinks they are. Read the following section carefully. If you have a habit of doing any of these things or something else that may make you appear anxious or disinterested, you need to extinguish that behavior.

 ESSENTIAL

Participate in videotaped mock job interviews to help you become aware of your body language. Once you are able to see yourself interacting with others, you can work on extinguishing any undesirable behaviors.

Stay Calm . . . or at Least Look That Way

A job interview is very stressful for most people. Your anxiety may be brought on by the fact that a job interview is a very unnatural situation to be in. How often do you sit across from another person while he or she fires a series of questions at you?

It is disconcerting to be put under a microscope by another person, especially when your livelihood may depend on the outcome of that person's research. Since one of your goals on a job interview is to appear confident, the last thing you want to do is let your body language betray your anxiety.

 FACT

Most people have some sort of behavior that appears when they are feeling anxious. One person may twirl the end of her hair or chew her bottom lip, another may wring his hands, and someone else may twist a ring around her finger or play with a pendant. Try to identify your own individual anxious behavior and keep it in check during the interview.

What to Do with Your Hands and Arms

Many people do not know what to do with their hands and arms during an interview. Should you clasp them together or keep them at your sides? Should you hold a pen to keep your hands occupied? Should you keep your arms folded across your chest?

The best thing to do with your hands is to let them rest in your lap. You may have them clasped together, as long as you don't clasp them too tightly and appear to be trying to hold them still. Folding your arms across your chest is often seen as an indication that you are closing yourself off or putting up a barrier. Since you want to appear open and approachable on a job interview, you should avoid doing that.

Holding a pen is not necessarily bad, but be careful not to fiddle with it. Remember not to point or clench your hands into fists. Also avoid covering your mouth with your hand or touching your face when you speak.

Make Eye Contact

If you have ever taken a public-speaking class, you no doubt discussed how important it is to make eye contact. If you avoid making eye contact, the interviewer may jump to the conclusion that you are not being truthful about something. That, of course, is the last thing you would want an interviewer to determine from your body language. She may also be wary of hiring someone who appears to have difficulty carrying on a conversation, which is another impression you need to avoid making.

 ESSENTIAL

If you tend to be shy or know that making eye contact tends to be a problem for you, you can practice making eye contact when you talk to people you are very comfortable with; for example, friends and family. Graduate to making eye contact with the cashier in the supermarket or the bank teller. Soon you should be able to accomplish this in all situations.

Sit Up Straight

How you sit during an interview is very important. Think back to when you were a child or a teenager and your parents and teachers told you to sit up straight. They were not kidding. Good posture helps you look confident. Slouching makes you look lazy and bored.

Sitting up straight also makes it easier to breathe, as any yoga instructor will tell you. When in a stressful situation, many people tend to forget to breathe. Then they let out a huge sigh when they remember. This is not a good idea during an interview.

It is preferable to keep your feet flat on the floor, but you can also have them crossed at the ankles. Do not cross your legs at the knee or have your ankle resting on your opposite knee. You should lean forward slightly. This shows that you are an eager participant in the conversation.

The Handshake

Another important thing to think about is the handshake. The opportunity for a handshake presents itself at two points in a job interview. One such juncture is when you first meet the interviewer. The other is at the end of the interview when you are getting ready to leave.

The moment when a handshake can take place can be somewhat awkward; for instance, if you put out your hand and the gesture is not reciprocated. However, if the interviewer puts out her hand and you are not ready to shake her hand at that moment, you will be putting her in an awkward situation. That is certainly something you want to avoid.

Therefore, while you do not want to initiate the handshake, you can make sure you are ready for it by keeping your right hand free at your side, ready to move into the handshake position. Avoid holding anything in your right hand as you enter and leave the office. When you do shake hands, your handshake should be firm, which demonstrates that you are confident.

 FACT

Many men who have no problem shaking the hand of another man get all wishy-washy when it comes time to shake hands with a woman. While it is true that a woman's hands may be more delicate than a man's hands, it is unlikely that your handshake will cause any damage. If you think it might, then you need to loosen up—whether it is a man's or a woman's hand you are shaking.

Making Your Exit

Just as your arrival at the interview provides you with your first opportunity to make a good impression, your exit provides you with the chance to make a lasting one. What you do at this point may be what sticks in the interviewer's mind it comes to making a decision about who to hire. Make sure you end on a positive note.

Do You Have Any Questions?

At the end of the interview, the interviewer will usually ask you if you have any questions. "No" is not a good answer. This is your chance to become a proactive part of the job interview, so don't waste it. The purpose of the questions you ask is twofold. They should indicate your interest in the job. They should also help you learn as much as you can to help you make an informed decision if you are offered the job. You should come to the interview with a list of prepared questions to ask the interviewer.

You can ask the interviewer to clarify the job duties or explain the chain of command. You can also ask him for more information about something he mentioned during the interview. You will find more questions you can ask in Chapter 14.

 ALERT!

When asking the employer questions at the end of your interview, you should not ask questions about salary, vacations, and benefits. All of these topics are best left for when the employer offers you the job. Not only is it considered to be more polite, but you will also be in a better position to negotiate once the employer knows she wants you to work for her.

Ask for the Job

Don't forget to ask for the job before you leave. Most people neglect to do this. They may not want to appear overly eager. However, the interviewer is not a mind reader. If you do not let him know you want the job, he may assume you do not want it.

You do not have to come out and say, "I want the job." You can instead say, "Based on what we discussed today, I think I would be a perfect fit for this job. When can I expect to hear from you?" This statement not only expresses your interest in the job, but also gives you the opportunity to reiterate that you are qualified to fill the position.

Before you leave, do not forget to say goodbye to the interviewer. Tell him it was nice to meet with him. As you did when you first began, be ready to shake the interviewer's hand if he extends it.

Interviewing over a Meal

When you find out your interview is going to take place over a meal, you may get indigestion before you even begin to eat. It is not enough worrying about impressing a potential employer with your words and avoiding any revealing body language. Now you also have to worry about using the right fork, not spilling soup on yourself, and not having food stuck between your teeth. Here are some tips that will help you survive the lunch (or dinner or breakfast) interview.

Sitting Down at the Table

When you arrive at the table, wait for everyone to sit down before you do, unless of course someone signals you to sit down first. After you sit down at the table, you should place your napkin on your lap. Generally you want to wait for your host to do this first. If the napkin is a large dinner-style one, you should fold it in half. If it is a small luncheon-style napkin, you can unfold it completely.

There may be a basket of bread on the table. If it is in front of you, offer it to your dining companions before you help yourself.

If it is not in front of you, wait until others have helped themselves before you ask someone to pass it to you. Do not reach in front of anyone or across the table to get it.

Place bread on your bread plate, which should be the smallest plate at your setting. Use your butter knife, or your regular knife if you do not have a butter knife, to place a piece of butter on your bread plate. Then break off a bite-sized piece of bread, apply the butter to it, and eat that piece. Do not butter an entire slice of bread or roll at once and proceed to eat it like a sandwich.

 FACT

Place settings will often include a variety of utensils. Many people are confused about what to use first, next, and so forth. The rule of thumb is to start furthest away from your plate and work your way in.

What to Order

When the waiter arrives to take drink orders, make yours a soda or water. While an alcoholic beverage may calm you down, it may also loosen you up—too much. If your host orders a bottle of wine for the table, refusing to have some may appear rude. In that case, allow the waiter to pour some for you, but sip it slowly.

When it comes time to order your meal, choose wisely. Stay away from any messy foods. Spaghetti is out. Avoid foods that tend to get stuck in your teeth, like spinach or poppy seeds. Choose something that is moderately priced. Your prospective employer is footing the bill and you do not want to look greedy.

The Meal

When the food begins to arrive, wait until everyone is served before you begin eating. When cutting up your food, use both your knife and fork to cut off one piece at a time. Do not hold your knife in your hand while you are eating and do not put a used utensil down on the table. Place your knife on your plate until you are ready to use it again.

Use your napkin to remove any crumbs from your face. Remember to dab and not wipe. When you are done eating, place your napkin on the table. It should be folded neatly, not crumpled up. Then politely wait for everyone else to finish.

 ESSENTIAL

Carry a travel-size toothbrush and toothpaste with you to use after the meal. You should be able to find a compact model that will fit in your purse or pocket so that if you suspect you have food stuck between your teeth, you can go to the restroom to remove it.

Don't Talk with Your Mouth Full

With your table manners in order, you can begin dealing with questions. The biggest question on your mind may be "How do I eat and answer questions at the same time?" With the finesse of a dentist, your interviewer may have a knack for asking you questions just as you put each forkful of food into your mouth. No matter how much you want to answer her question, remember what your mom told you—don't talk with your mouth full. It only takes a few seconds to chew and swallow, although it may seem like an eternity to you. Also remember to completely answer each question before you continue to eat.

Finishing Up

When your host places her napkin on the table, it is a signal that the meal is done. You do not want to keep her there any longer than is necessary. This may or may not mean the end of the interview. Follow the interviewer's lead. When the interview is over, do what you would do at the end of a regular interview, with the addition of thanking her for the meal.

Interviewing in a Foreign Country

In today's global marketplace it is possible that you could wind up interviewing for a job in a foreign country. If this happens, you will have to learn about the culture of that country since a breach of etiquette could be interpreted as rudeness. You will have to learn about things like the proper way to greet someone, whether it is appropriate to look someone in the eye, and good table manners. The following guidelines will get you started.

 QUESTION?

Where can I find out more about the rules of etiquette for a specific country?
Many books have been written about cross-cultural rules of etiquette. Check your local library or the Internet for specific information on the country you are visiting. Appendix B includes a list of resources.

Be sure you know the proper method of greeting for the country you are visiting. In some cultures, people bow when they meet one another. To complicate matters further, different bows mean different things. You should make a point of learning the meaning of each one in order to avoid making any missteps.

Certain body language, while acceptable in one culture, may be considered rude in another. For example, it is considered rude to look someone directly in the eye in some countries. What is appropriate for men in a particular culture may be inappropriate for women.

If you are interviewing in another country, it is very likely that you will be faced with an interview over a meal. You may be served unfamiliar foods, some of which you cannot even imagine eating. When torn between being polite and being nauseated, it is okay not to eat something you find repulsive. However, you should accept what is offered. You should also become familiar with the table manners that are appropriate in that culture.

CHAPTER 3

Revealing Your Personality

YOU'VE MET THE INTERVIEWER, shaken her hand, and now you're settling into your seat. Okay, bring it on. You're ready for anything she's going to ask. You can talk about each job you've had, your skills, and your accomplishments. Suddenly you find yourself barraged with a bunch of personal questions. The interviewer is asking about things that seem to have nothing to do with work. Why does she need to know so much about you?

Why the Personal Questions?

Why would an employer want to know what you like doing for fun, your strengths and weaknesses, and even how many siblings you grew up with? Then comes the most dreaded question: "So, tell me about yourself." Your heart begins to pound so loudly, you're sure the interviewer can hear it. "Tell you about myself? Have you got a few hours?"

Be assured the interviewer usually doesn't want to know all the private details of your life. As a matter of fact, she doesn't have the right to ask for that kind of information. (More on that in Chapter 12.) What a prospective employer is interested in learning about are your personal qualities, or your character traits. This information will help her decide whether to hire you.

Basically, the prospective employer wants to know if you have what it takes to work at his company. Yes, you may have the skills and experience, but do you have the personality? Aspects of your personality are a strong indication of whether you will make a good employee. The interviewer wants to know whether or not you procrastinate, are discreet, and are a team player. He wants to know if you work well on your own, how you make decisions, handle stress, and solve problems.

Before beginning the interviewing process, a hiring manager may have gone through hundreds of resumes looking for candidates who have the skills and experience required for the job in question. The interviewer's job now is to be a detective. He wants to know what makes you a better choice than another candidate with the same experience and skills.

An interviewer will try to learn about your personality by either asking you directly or by asking you questions that get you to reveal this information. Consider every question the interviewer asks very carefully. Try to figure out what he is really asking.

 ALERT!

Don't reveal more about yourself than is necessary during a job interview. While you should be honest with the interviewer, don't tell her more than she needs to know. Revealing too much information can get you into trouble.

Now, back to the dreaded question: "Tell me about yourself." The interviewer doesn't want your memoirs. The rule of thumb is to keep it simple. The interviewer is interested only in knowing whether you have the skills and qualities necessary to fulfill the requirements of the position you are interviewing for. Interviewees sometimes make the mistake of revealing too much about themselves at this point when all the prospective employer really wants to know is "Can you do the job?" and "Will you fit in here?"

Q. Tell me about yourself.

A. I attended Ace Business College, where I earned my associate's degree in office technology five years ago. I started working as a library clerk right after I graduated, and after a year I was promoted to assistant circulation manager. I helped the library switch over to a new circulation system about two years ago. I was part of the team that selected the new system and I helped train our department in its use. In addition to my technical skills, I am adept at troubleshooting. I also work well with customers, helping to solve any problems that arise. I'm now ready to take on a job with more responsibility and I know I will make a great circulation manager.

This candidate tells the interviewer about his skills and experience and shows why he is qualified for the job. He doesn't wander off course, revealing information that is irrelevant. The answer is relatively short and, more importantly, to the point.

Never say: "I was born in Wisconsin, one of three children. I did well in school. I was on the football team and editor of my school newspaper. I moved to Chicago to go to college and . . ." The interviewer doesn't want your life story. Keep your answer limited to the parts that will affect your suitability for the job.

Q. Do you work well on your own?

A. Yes, I do. I'm very focused and efficient.

This is a very simple and honest answer. Most jobs will require you to work on your own sometimes, if not all the time.

Never say: "I would much rather work on my own." Many jobs also require you to be part of a team at times. Don't volunteer information that makes you seem difficult to work with—just answer the question.

Q. What do you consider to be your biggest weakness?

A. I am very dedicated to my job and I expect the same level of dedication from other people. Not everyone feels the same way about work and sometimes my expectations are too high.

Wouldn't every boss love such a dedicated employee? This interviewee knew she had to find a weakness that her prospective employer would see as a strength. Another option is to pick a weakness that is somewhat innocuous.

Never say: "I don't have any weaknesses." Oh, come on. Who's going to believe that?

Q. What would your friends say is your biggest weakness?

A. Whenever my friends and I travel together, I do a lot of advanced planning. Most of my travel companions appreciate it, but some find it annoying. We just went to the Southwest, and three months before we were going I had already put together a list of all the things we had to see. I kept them going all day long every day.

This candidate chooses to talk about something that could be perceived as a weakness but that also demonstrates his skills. By giving this answer he demonstrates three skills—planning, research, and strong leadership qualities. Some of his friends may not appreciate his advanced planning, which is why he considers this a weakness.

Never say: "I never see my friends because I'm always working." You know what they say about all work and no play. A little time away from the office is good for everyone.

Q. How do you handle success?

A. I give myself a quick pat on the back and move on to the next project. Of course, I take the time to figure out what helped me succeed and use that experience to help me the next time.

This prospective employee takes appropriate pride in her success, while ascribing to the old adage "Don't rest on your laurels." She also learns from her experience.

Never say: "I make sure everyone knows about it. If I don't brag about my own success, who will?" That's true, but there are more subtle ways of getting the word out. Besides, if she's so busy bragging, who's doing all her work?

Q. How do you handle failure?

A. I give myself a short time to feel sad, but I don't dwell on it. Who has time for that? Without spending too much energy on it, I do always try to figure out where things went wrong. If I don't do that, I won't know what I need to do to succeed next time.

This isn't someone who wastes any time feeling sorry for himself. He's also smart enough to learn from his mistakes.

Never say: "I never fail, so I don't have to handle it." Everyone has failures, so the interviewer can only assume this candidate is lying or joking. Either way, he may be able to count this interview among his failures.

Q. What are your long-term goals?

A. I want to move into a supervisory position eventually. I know that will take time and hard work, but it is something I expect to achieve.

That's a good answer as long as the interviewer isn't the only supervisor. (The interviewee doesn't want to seem as if he's after the interviewer's job.) It's important to emphasize not only that you have goals, but also that you are willing to do the work to reach them.

Never say: "I want to run this place." Wait. Doesn't the interviewer run this place?

Q. What are your short-term goals?

A. I want to work for a company that is growing, in a position that allows me to use my skills to help that growth. I know your company is trying to expand into the teen market. My experience selling to that market will help your company reach its goals.

This interviewee's goals are aligned with those of the company. By giving an example of how she will help the company meet its goals, she has forced the employer to visualize her as an employee. This answer also shows that the interviewee took the time to research the company before her appointment.

Never say: "I plan to begin working on my MBA as soon as possible." While this interviewee is clearly ambitious, she hasn't shown how her goals have anything to do with the job that she's interviewing for.

Q. Do you prefer to work alone or as part of a team?

A. Each situation is different. Having a team to collaborate with works better for some projects, while it's best for one person to work on other projects. I enjoy being part of a team, but I can work independently, too.

This interviewer shows that she's flexible and can adapt to working in either situation.

Never say: "Teams are clearly a better use of resources. I'm a team player all the way." It's important to show flexibility because most jobs require you to be able to work independently at least some of the time.

Q. What do you consider to be your greatest strength?

A. My greatest strength is my ability to see a project through from its inception to its completion. Each project I am assigned is important to me and I always make sure it gets the appropriate amount of attention.

Notice the interviewee said each project gets the "appropriate amount of attention" and not "all my attention." She clearly knows that not all projects need the same amount of attention and indicates that she knows how to prioritize.

Never say: "I'm a hard worker and I always get to work on time." Getting to work on time is expected of all workers, as is being a hard worker.

Q. How many siblings did you grow up with and how did that influence who you are today?

A. *Answer 1:* I grew up as one of five children. When you grow up in such a large family, you must function as a team. Everyone takes on different responsibilities. Because my parents were so busy all the time, I also learned to be very independent. Or, *Answer 2:* I grew up as an only child. I was very independent. When I got to school I had to learn how to share my toys with other kids. It was a difficult lesson, but it helped me become a better team player.

The interviewee, regardless of the size family in which he grew up, shows that he can work alone or as part of a team.

Never say: *Answer 1:* "I grew up with five brothers and sisters. It was always really noisy. I think that's why I love being alone now." *Answer 2:* "I was an only child. I got so used to being alone that I really like it better that way." Uh-oh. Neither answer shows that the interviewee is flexible enough to be a team player when he needs to be.

Q. Do you like to take risks or are you cautious?

A. I'll take risks but I always proceed with caution, so I guess I fall somewhere in between. I like to see what my odds are before I take a risk. I also want to know what I stand to gain or lose.

This candidate is a careful decision-maker who isn't afraid to take risks if there is a high probability of success. He also wants to make sure the risk is worth taking. He's not a gambler, but he's not afraid to take chances when it's appropriate to do so.

Never say: "I'm a risk-taker" or "I'm cautious." Most employers want someone with a combination of these traits.

Q. Do others think of you as a leader?

A. I believe those who have seen me in action are confident in my ability to lead them. Whenever we had to work in committees in my marketing class, my fellow committee members always chose me to be chairperson.

This answer is honest and to the point. Although she is interviewing for her first job, she is able to draw on her college experience to come up with an example.

Never say: "I lead and others follow." Confidence is good, but cockiness is not.

Q. Do you consider yourself a leader?

A. I am willing to take on responsibility, I am persuasive, and I can delegate. All these qualities make me a good leader. If a situation calls for someone to take charge, I will certainly step forward.

This interviewer states the qualities that make her a good leader but knows to tread lightly here. She wants to show she can evaluate the needs of each situation and step forward if necessary, while making it clear she's a team player.

Never say: "Yes. I like being in charge." This candidate doesn't tell the interviewer why he is qualified to lead, but sounds determined to take a leadership position no matter who he steps on.

Ⓔ ALERT!

Don't give answers that are too short or don't fully explain things. Try to figure out why the interviewer has asked a particular question and answer the question with that in mind.

Q. How do you handle pressure?

A. I take a deep breath and figure out what needs to be done. Then I take care of it. One day my current boss came to me with a big research project that needed to be completed by the following morning. It was already 4 P.M. I rounded up my team and divided the project among us. We got it done with enough time to get home to sleep for a few hours before returning to work in the morning.

This interviewee has a strategy in place for dealing with pressure. She demonstrates how she dealt with one difficult situation using some valuable skills, including the abilities to delegate and work as part of a team.

Never say: "I work best under pressure." That may be true, but this interviewee needs to elaborate.

Q. Are you a procrastinator or do you like to get things done?

A. Though I've been known to procrastinate on occasion, I don't make a habit of it. When someone hands me a project that needs to be done in a timely fashion, I will get it done.

Who hasn't procrastinated on occasion? What matters is that this candidate knows the difference between a project that can wait and one that needs to be done right away, and can finish the pressing ones in time to meet deadlines.

Never say: "I never procrastinate." Do you believe her?

Q. What pet peeves do you have about coworkers?

A. Too much negativity always bothers me. I think if you're going to complain you should be able to offer some solutions to fix the things you think are wrong.

By giving this answer, this candidate is saying, "I'm not a negative person. If I see a problem, I figure out how to fix it."

Never say: "I say live and let live. They can do what they want—it doesn't bother me." It's virtually impossible to spend forty hours a week with a group of people and still get along perfectly with them. This candidate seems to be too easygoing—he'd rather let things slide than deal with them.

Q. We're not one of those companies that do things the same way year after year. How do you react to change?

A. When appropriate, change is important. For example, when I heard about a new payroll system at a conference last year, I did a little investigating, found out it was better than what we were using, and recommended we move over to it.

This interviewee has shown that she doesn't shy away from change, even providing a good example of how she initiated it at work. She has also shown that she doesn't jump into change just for the sake of doing something different, but rather, does her homework first.

Never say: "Change is great. Without it I get bored." Does that change include finding a new job every other year?

Q. What is the best money you ever spent?

A. I really wanted to go to a school out of state, but my parents couldn't afford to send me, so I took a year off after high school and worked two jobs to earn enough money to cover the difference between the local school they could afford and the one I wanted to go to. It was a great experience. Besides, getting a great education while living away from home taught me to be independent.

This man knows how to reach his goals and he's not afraid of hard work.

Never say: "I got this awesome new sports car. It is so sharp, a real chick magnet." Not only does this answer sound immature, it may make the interviewer question the applicant's priorities. Does he really want to hire someone who will be chasing all the women in the office?

Q. What was your worst purchase?

A. I'm almost embarrassed to admit this. There were these boots that were popular a few years ago. They literally cost everything I earned working during the summer. I bought them, they lasted one season, and then they were out of style.

So you spent all your earnings on a pair of boots? That's pretty innocuous as far as frivolous purchases go. The interviewee makes sure to point out that it happened a few years ago when she didn't know any better, and that she has learned from the mistake.

Never say: "I bought my girlfriend this really expensive engagement ring and then we broke up because she was seeing my best friend behind my back." This answer reveals way too much personal information.

Q. What is the last thing you read?

A. I just finished the latest book on management techniques by Joseph Brown. I'm always trying to keep up with the latest literature in the field.

Reading is a great way to keep up with changes in one's field and this interviewee knows it. She proves that her interest in the field goes beyond just the nine-to-five job.

Never say: "My job keeps me so busy I really don't have time to read." Even if you don't have time to read for pleasure, you should have time to keep up with your professional literature if you want to be seen as a dedicated applicant.

Ⓔ QUESTION?

Should I discuss my personal taste in books?
You should try to keep your answers related to your career. When your prospective employer asks what you have read lately, stick to professional literature.

Q. Do you have any hobbies?

A. I love woodworking. I've made tables, chairs, and a bookshelf. I love the satisfaction I get from taking a few pieces of wood and turning them into something I, or someone else, can use.

This answer shows that the interviewee can see a project through from beginning to end.

Never say: "Who has time for hobbies?" A successful job candidate must show that he or she is well rounded.

Q. How do you make decisions?

A. I evaluate the situation before I decide what I need to do. If there is someone who has had experience with similar situations, I'm not afraid to ask for advice.

This interviewee isn't going to make a decision without considering it carefully. She is also very resourceful—seeking advice from people with more experience is always a good idea.

Never say: "I usually go with my first instinct." This interviewee clearly doesn't put a lot of thought into things, including this answer.

Q. What do you, as an employee, owe your boss and what does your boss owe you?

A. I owe my boss hard work, respect, and honesty. My boss owes me respect, honesty, and recognition for my hard work.

In a world were honesty isn't always easy to find, this prospective employee is promising a rare commodity. The same can be said for respect. Hard work is a must, of course, but some employees only do the minimum. She is also clear about what she expects from her prospective employer.

Never say: "I owe my employer everything. I'm at my boss's disposal. What do I expect in return? My salary." This may be every employer's dream employee . . . if it were true.

 FACT

Interviewers are usually pretty perceptive. They know when a job candidate says something that is too good to be true. Keep your answers realistic.

Q. I see that you worked full-time while attending graduate school. How did you manage to balance everything?

A. It was difficult, but I managed not to fall behind at work or school. I worked five full days a week and took classes two evenings a week. I studied on the other three nights and on the weekends.

This candidate shows that he was determined to complete his degree but not at the expense of his job.

Never say: "I walked around exhausted all the time." This doesn't answer the interviewer's question or tell her anything about the candidate other than that he doesn't handle stress well.

Ⓔ ALERT!

> Listen carefully during the interview. Ask for clarification if you need it. You won't be able to answer a question properly unless you understand what the interviewer is asking you.

Q. How do you feel about lying?

A. I think lying has the potential to get you into trouble. It's much better to be honest and up front. If you are caught in a lie, the person you lied to will not have a reason to trust you in the future.

This interviewee doesn't just say lying is bad, but he also backs up his opinion by giving a negative result of lying.

Never say: "I never lie." That wasn't the question.

Q. Did you enjoy school as a child?

A. Not really. I always got good grades but I think I was bored. Most teachers just talked at us. My favorite classes were the ones where group discussions happened frequently.

Someone who didn't like school won't necessarily be a bad employee. This interviewee is honest, and gives a reason for the way he feels.

Never say: "I hated school. I couldn't wait to get out of there. All those teachers telling me what to do drove me crazy." Even though this interviewee had the same experience as the previous one, he is a little too vehement about his feelings without giving an explanation.

Q. Can you describe your ideal work environment?

A. I want to work in an environment where I can use my presentation skills to help the company increase its client roster. It's important that I work in a fast-paced environment because I like being busy. I want to work somewhere where employees are recognized for their contributions.

Based on some research, she is able to describe both the job that she's interviewing for and her potential employer. By showing that her ideal fits with what the job requires, she shows that she is the perfect fit for the position.

Never say: "I want to work in a clean office with good lighting. I prefer to be on a lower floor. I really don't like cubicles." Even if this candidate had done her homework, and this was an accurate description of her potential employer's offices, this answer doesn't say anything about the job or her qualifications for it.

Q. If you won a million dollars, what would you do?

A. I know some people would say they'd quit their jobs and go off to some island, but they haven't considered the fact that a million dollars won't take you very far. Besides, I find this type of work fulfilling. I'd probably take a nice vacation and buy a new car. Then I'd go back to work and invest the rest of the money.

This interviewee is practical. A million dollars wouldn't actually guarantee a work-free life.

Never say: "I would quit my job and move to the South of France." Aside from the fact that this person is saying he'd leave his job if something better came along, this person isn't very practical.

Q. Why did you choose this career?

A. When I started college, I wasn't sure what I wanted to do. I visited the career office and they gave me some self-assessment tests. Based on the results, they gave me a list of careers that might be suitable and told me how to research them. I did, and this is what I thought I'd like best.

Great answer. This is someone who knows what steps to take to make an important decision.

Never say: "My parents had a friend in the field and he thought I'd be good at it." That is the wrong way to make a career choice. It may make the interviewer wonder how this person will make other decisions.

Chapter CHAPTER 4

Discussing Your Skills and Abilities

YOUR SKILLS—that's why they pay you the big bucks. Well, maybe not the big bucks, but it is why they pay you anything at all. Who you are as a person, as discussed in Chapter 3, will help an employer decide if you have the characteristics that make you a good fit for his or her company. To fit into a particular job, you'll also need a certain set of skills. Your skills represent your ability to do the job at hand.

Hard Skills

Skills can be divided into two categories: hard skills and soft skills. Hard skills are the technical skills that define your job. Simply put, a baker must know how to bake, an accountant must know how to balance the books, a nurse must know how to care for patients, and a teacher must know how to teach. Of course, these basic skills can be broken down into more specific hard skills. For example, an accountant might be skilled in the following areas: accounts receivable, accounts payable, auditing, taxation, and payroll.

As anyone who has ever worked can tell you, what you do at work can vary greatly from your formal job description. In addition to your regular job duties, you may be required to write, make presentations, use a computer, or do research. These are also hard skills, but are not necessarily part of your "official" job description. Nevertheless, you will be required to be proficient in these skills and your prospective employer will want you to prove this to him by drawing on specific examples of how you have used your skills.

 FACT

Hard skills are often those skills that you learned in school or through some other formal training or prior work experience. Typically you will choose a job based on the hard skills you possess, but some employers are willing to let you pick them up on the job.

Soft Skills

Soft skills are those skills that you need to have in order to excel at work in general. These are very wide-ranging skills. They aren't specific to any occupation, but instead are the things that enhance your performance regardless of what your actual job is. Examples of these soft skills include decision-making, time management, delegating, multitasking, and problem solving.

 ESSENTIAL

When you prepare for a job interview, make a list of all your soft skills and all your hard skills. Think of specific examples of when you've had to use each of them, especially those that are most relevant to the job you are interviewing for.

Remember, when the job interviewer asks whether you have a particular skill, she doesn't want a simple yes or no answer. She wants to know how you obtained the skill, how you've used the skill, and how you plan to use it to benefit her company.

Skills You Haven't Used Professionally

You may be concerned if you have a particular skill, but you haven't actually used it on the job. You may have learned the skill in school and never used it at work. If this is the case, can you think of a time you used that skill for an extracurricular activity or in another situation on your own time?

 FACT

> People develop skills in a variety of ways that are unrelated to paid employment. You may have learned a new skill when you participated in a school club or organization. You may use certain skills in running your household or in your volunteer work.

You may have picked up the skill from a volunteer experience, in which case you never actually got paid to use that skill. If so, you should discuss using the skill as if you used it on a job, talking about how it benefited the organization you were involved with. If you can't even rely on examples of unpaid experience, at least come up with an example of how you would be able to use the skill to benefit the employer and his company.

Q. How well do you think you perform as a manager?

A. I've never officially had the title "manager," but I've often had to act as manager when my boss is out of the office. She's always been very pleased with the job I've done.

This candidate doesn't let the fact that he's never actually had the title of manager stop him from explaining why he can do the job.

Never say: "Well, since I've never been a manager, I don't know." If you've had some managerial experience, even if it was just supervising a single project, you should talk about that. If you've had no managerial experience, then you can talk about it hypothetically.

Q. How are your presentation skills? How do you prepare for presentations?

A. I didn't always like making presentations, but since I had to make a lot of them on my last two jobs, I've gotten very good at it. I do a lot of research before any presentation. I try to find out as much as possible about the client, the market they are trying to reach, their competitors, and the industry. Sometimes, if the budget allows for it, I hire an expert to help me with the research.

This client answered honestly. He knows it's not that unusual to dislike presentations, so he's not afraid to admit that. It also gives him the opportunity to show off his experience and how it has gotten him over his fear. In addition, he knows the importance of having good information and knows what resources he needs to use to get it.

Never say: "I love making presentations. The only problem I have is that I find if I'm too prepared, my presentation sounds scripted." This candidate would have benefited from a little preparation to get him through the interview.

Q. How do your skills relate to this job?

A. I am very organized, I work well on a team, and I have very good communication skills. Although I haven't worked in this field before, I know these skills will make me a valuable employee.

Although this applicant is new to the field, she has some very desirable skills, which she makes a point of letting the interviewer know.

Never say: "I haven't worked in this field before, but I'm a fast learner." This candidate makes the mistake of dwelling on his lack of skill instead of his strengths.

Q. How do you solve problems?

A. First I assess the problem. Then I figure out what I need to do to solve it. For example, last month we were hosting a conference. Our receptionist, who was supposed to greet attendees, called in sick. With the conference scheduled to start in an hour we had to do something fast. I quickly went through a list of employees who might be able to handle hosting duties, but found that each was involved in some other aspect of the conference. I called my contact at a local temp agency, after getting my boss's approval, and we had a replacement host shortly.

After telling the interviewer how he solves problems, this applicant gives a real-life example.

Never say: "If you do your job well, you shouldn't have any problems." This candidate is in a state of denial.

Q. Have you ever been in a situation where the majority disagrees with you? What did you do?

A. I haven't been in that situation, but here's what I would do if I were: First I would listen to why the majority felt the way they did. Then I'd have to decide whether I needed to reconsider my position. If I still felt strongly about it after hearing their side, I would try to persuade them.

This candidate knew better than to dismiss the question just because he couldn't draw on his experience to answer it. Rather than make something up, he tells the interviewer what he would do if he were in that situation. His answer shows that he is flexible enough to try to see things differently, but strong enough in his convictions to not automatically go with the crowd.

Never say: "We were designing our new brochure and I thought yellow and purple would look great. Everyone else wanted to go with burgundy and blue. Since I had the most seniority, they had to do it my way." Flexible? No. A bully? Maybe.

Q. Please describe your work in the military.

A. As an Army finance specialist, I audited financial records, disbursed cash and checks, and recorded details of financial transactions using standard forms.

This job candidate, an Army veteran, clearly states what her military work involved. Since military job descriptions are often different than civilian job descriptions, it was not only important for her to state what her title was, but to also describe her duties.

Never say: "I was a finance specialist."

Q. How are you at delegating?

A. I have such a high level of trust in my staff members that delegating to them is easy. I know each person's strengths and weaknesses, so I can easily decide who can handle what jobs and duties. I try to give people projects that challenge them but won't defeat them.

This candidate is obviously a good manager. He puts a lot of thought into how to delegate responsibilities and makes a point of knowing his staff very well.

Never say: "I'm good at delegating. I don't want to do all the work myself." This guy just sounds lazy.

Q. Tell me about a crisis you encountered at work and how you handled it.

A. Last year a virus was causing our computers to send out thousands of e-mail messages to our clients. We were being inundated with angry phone calls before we even knew what was going on. Our technical support person was on vacation, so I made a few phone calls and found someone to fix the problem. Then I drafted an apology that was sent out by e-mail to our clients.

This answer is good because the candidate clearly describes the problem and gives specifics on how she solved it. In addition, the crisis is one that could have caused her boss to lose clients, something that would strike fear into the hearts of most employers, including the one interviewing her.

Never say: "My assistant called in sick right before I was leaving on vacation. I was counting on her to run some errands for me. Since she wasn't there I had to get one of the interns to do it." This candidate is resourceful, but he shouldn't have had anyone running his errands on company time.

Q. How do you manage your time?

A. I prioritize my work. I figure out what needs to get done first, next, and so on. Then I calculate how much time I will need to spend on each activity or project. I set a schedule for myself and get going.

This applicant has a plan. He knows how to prioritize and apportion the proper amount of time to each activity.

Never say: "I get to work early and stay late to get everything done." This answer doesn't show that the applicant can manage his time. Rather, he can get everything done as long as he works long hours (which may cost the employer extra overtime).

Q. We use PQR Write to lay out our brochures. Do you know how to use it?

A. I use a program that is very similar to that. I also have a friend who uses PQR and I'm sure he'd be happy to give me a crash course. I know I can learn it by the time I start work.

There are so many software programs out there, it would be impossible to know how to use all of them. This candidate knew better than to lie about her experience and instead told her prospective employer how she would get the skills she needs. Notice how she says she'll know the program by the time "I start work," not "if I get this job."

Never say: "No, I only feel comfortable with Super Page. Couldn't I just keep using that?"

Q. Are you computer literate?

A. I'm proficient in several programs, including WordRight, Bottom Line, and Quick Pages.

Instead of just saying she is computer literate, this candidate goes beyond that and discusses which software programs she knows how to use. The programs she chooses to highlight are those that are relevant to the job that she's applying for.

Never say: "I know how to go online and I can use a word processor." This candidate should be more specific, making a point of mentioning programs that are specific to his field.

Q. We handle a large volume of tax returns here. How has your experience prepared you for this?

A. During college, I participated in the IRS's Volunteer Income Tax Assistance program. For two nights a week, from February through April, I spent a few hours preparing individual tax returns in a public library near my college. I prepared about five returns each evening.

This job candidate, although he doesn't have professional experience, is able to demonstrate his skills through his volunteer experience. He speaks about the number of tax returns he processed, demonstrating that he can work efficiently.

Never say: "I do a few returns each year but I'm sure I'll be able to handle the volume." This candidate, even though he doesn't have practical experience with preparing a large volume of tax returns, needs to find some past experience that proves to the interviewer that he can handle a large volume of work in general.

Q. Have you ever had to juggle two or more projects at the same time?

A. That happened all the time on my last job. Several months ago, I was in the midst of working on one huge project for one of my bosses, when my other boss came to me with another project that needed to be completed in two days. After evaluating the second project, I realized I could complete it in a day. Since I still had about a week before the deadline for the first project, I decided to get started on the second one. I completed it by the end of the next day and went back to my first project.

The interviewer asked for an example and this candidate gave one. He demonstrates how his ability to prioritize helped him.

Never say: "I can't think of any right now. Can I get back to you on that one?" The interviewee should have prepared for this in advance.

Q. What does your desk look like?

A. I try to keep it organized, which is not always an easy feat with the volume of work that comes across it. I find that if I know where everything is I can work much more efficiently.

This is a vague question, but this interviewee has quickly figured out what the interviewer was looking for. She gives a realistic answer. She knows the importance of having an organized work area, but also knows that it's sometimes difficult to keep it that way, especially when you're keeping busy.

Never say: "It's brown and made of wood." This isn't quite what the interviewer wanted to know.

Q. We need someone with very strong auditing skills. Do you qualify?

A. Yes I do. As a staff accountant at Crabgrass and Weed, I regularly performed audits of our clients' financial records. I examined financial source documents to make sure procedures were followed correctly and generated adjusting journal entries as needed. I also prepared final reports for our clients.

The interviewee specifically states how her experience has prepared her for this position.

Never say: "Yes, I do. I had some auditing responsibilities on my last job." This applicant has the skills necessary, but she needs to elaborate on them.

Q. How do you take direction?

A. I think the ability to listen is one of the most important skills for anyone to have. I always make sure to pay attention to what my supervisor is saying and then ask any questions I have. I find out when the project must be completed and if there are any special issues I must be attentive to.

This candidate demonstrates that she has no problem taking direction from her superiors, or for that matter, following those directions.

Never say: "Why should that matter? Won't I be in charge?" Even if this person is applying for a high-level position, he will still have to answer to someone, unless he plans to buy the company.

Q. As assistant to the director of human resources, employees will come to you if they feel their supervisor has discriminated against them in some way. How will you handle these complaints?

A. As an HR professional I know the importance of being well versed in the laws that affect the workplace. First, I will interview the employee, asking for an explanation of exactly what happened. Then, I'll interview the supervisor and get his or her side of the story.

This candidate will take a balanced look at the situation. He will evaluate it using his knowledge of employment law and then try to solve the problem.

Never say: "I'd refer it to our company's legal counsel." This applicant needs to show he knows how to deal with issues that regularly occur before dumping them in someone else's lap.

Q. What skills can you bring to our school?

A. As you can see from my resume, I've been a teacher at the Parkside School for five years. I've taught second and third grades. I form strong relationships with my students. They trust me, as do their parents. Many view me as a strict teacher, and in fact, I am an excellent classroom manager. My students know what I expect of them and are generally very cooperative. I am a skilled communicator. I structure my lessons so that I reach all my students. My classes always perform well on statewide exams.

This applicant knows what skills make a successful teacher and she has shown that she possesses them all.

Never say: "I love kids and I'm a good teacher." This candidate needs to do more than state the obvious.

Q. As principal, the most frequent complaint I hear from parents is about teachers who don't maintain good communications with them. What have you done as a teacher to help maintain communication with parents of your students?

A. First of all, parents can reach me by e-mail, by sending in a note, or by telephone. I am not able to respond immediately, but I always get back to them before the end of the day. I encourage parents to come to the classroom to read to the children. I send home a "Dear Parents" letter every two weeks explaining what we've covered in the classroom during the prior two weeks and what we will be covering during the upcoming weeks.

This job candidate talks about what he is currently doing to maintain good communications with parents. Not only does he communicate with parents when he has an issue to discuss, he also keeps the lines of communication open.

Never say: "When there's a problem, I contact the parents immediately." The principal wants to know how this teacher communicates regularly, not only if there's something that needs to be discussed.

Q. Have you ever done therapy with a group before?

A. Yes, I have. When I worked at the University, I organized a support group for students coping with panic attacks. I met with them once a week. I also took over a support group for families of cancer patients when I worked at Old Hills Hospital.

This job candidate has given two examples that demonstrate her skills, even highlighting one that she organized.

Never say: "Yes, I have." Remember, you need to back this up with an example.

Q. You have many of the skills we're looking for. However, we also need someone with very strong sales skills. I don't see anything on your resume that indicates that you have that kind of experience.

A. Yes, it's true that I don't have any formal experience in sales. I do have some informal experience, however. I ran the book fair at my son's school for the past few years. I also sold jewelry that a friend made. We rented tables at craft fairs all over the region.

While a candidate can't make up experience, she should draw on unpaid or volunteer experience that demonstrates her skills.

Never say: "No, I don't have any sales experience, but I can learn." This candidate should try to find some past experience that demonstrates her skills. If she truly has no sales experience, she might consider the qualities that make a good salesperson and find a way to demonstrate that she has those qualities.

Q. We expect the executive director to handle a lot of fundraising. Do you have any experience with that?

A. Yes, I do. I spearheaded a campaign that raised over $10,000 for a small library for our members. I also run an annual campaign to raise money for our after-school center. Over the last five years, we've increased donations by about 6 percent each year.

This candidate quantifies his accomplishments. It's one way of saying here's what I did for my current employer and this is what I can do for you.

Never say: "I've done some fundraising on my job." This candidate needs to be more specific.

Q. Why should we hire you to be senior manager of our technical support department? You don't have any experience in technical support.

A. While I don't have any experience in technical support, I do have six years of experience in customer service and management. I know how important it is to provide a good experience for customers. It builds loyalty, which will keep them coming back. I've managed customer service departments with staffs that ranged from 15 to 100 employees.

Although this candidate's experience is not in technical support, he has managed departments that deal with consumer issues. He explains how that experience qualifies him for this position.

Never say: "I use computers all the time, so I know how to answer the questions we would get." Computer skills do not qualify this applicant for a managerial position.

Q. What is your management style?

A. I'm a hands-on manager. I dive right in and work alongside my employees. This not only sets a good example for them, but also helps keep me aware of everyone's strengths and weaknesses.

This interviewee knows how to keep people motivated. She provides a reason for having chosen that style.

Never say: "I'm very strict. I say how it gets done and when." Ruling with an iron fist does not lead to a satisfied staff.

Q. Are you good at doing research?

A. I haven't done a great deal of research at work, but I do a lot of it on my own. Before I make any major purchases, take any medication, or go on vacation, I do a lot of research. I'm very good at it. The librarians at my local library are a great resource, so I make sure to go to them when I need help.

It would have been nice if this job candidate could have drawn on work experience to highlight her research skills, but since she couldn't, she did the next best thing. She has given examples of what kind of research she has done and how she does it.

Never say: "I guess so. I like using the Net." An avid Internet user does not necessarily make a good researcher.

Q. As you know, this is a new programming director position. We're thinking about having the person in this position also handle promoting our programs. Is that something you can handle?

A. My primary responsibility as program director at the Art Council was program development. However, we had a very small staff, so I was usually responsible for promotion as well. I wrote press releases, designed print ads, and compiled mailing lists. This would be a great way to utilize some of my skills.

While highlighting his primary skill, program development, this applicant also draws upon some of his secondary responsibilities to explain why this job is a good fit.

Never say: "I would be thrilled to be doing publicity. That was my favorite part of my last job." The interviewer said that publicity *might* be part of this job. Would this candidate be disappointed and quit if it turned out not to be so?

Q. How do you think others rate you as a supervisor?

A. Turnover in my department since I was promoted to supervisor five years ago has decreased from 30 percent to 10 percent. The reason, I believe, is that I treat those who work under me fairly. When a big deadline is coming up, I'm right there working late with them and not heading out the door at 5 P.M. I've had employees tell me they appreciate that.

This candidate knows that saying she's highly regarded as a supervisor isn't enough. She needs to back up her claim, which she does by telling her prospective employer how much turnover in her department decreased. She goes on to tell the interviewer why she believes this is so.

Never say: "They think I'm a good supervisor. They never complain and they do what I tell them to do." There's more to being a good supervisor than this.

Q. What skills can you bring to the pediatric unit at St. Ernestine?

A. I worked with children for about eight years as an assistant nursery school teacher before going back to school to become a nurse. When I began nursing school, I knew I wanted to specialize in pediatrics. I relate well to children and they relate well to me. I am a compassionate, as well as skilled, nurse. I offer patients the comfort they need when they are terrified of being in the hospital.

This answer demonstrates the candidates experience working with children as well as his nursing skills.

Never say: "I've spent four years training to be a nurse."

Q. I see from your resume this isn't your first job working in a medical office. What skills did you pick up on your two previous jobs that you think would help you on this job?

A. When you described the job to me, you said you needed someone who was good with patients. You also said you wanted someone who knows a lot about the different insurance plans. My primary responsibility at both these jobs was billing. I had to deal with insurance companies every day. I found that if I learned how each one worked, it was a lot easier for the doctors in my practice to get paid and for patients to get reimbursed. I also worked at the reception desk at these jobs. Many patients who came in were clearly anxious. I was happy to be able to calm them down and hopefully offer some reassurance.

This candidate listened to what the employer said and was able to clearly state how her skills would fill this medical practice's needs.

Never say: "You wanted someone who is good with patients and insurance. That would be me." This candidate needs to elaborate.

Q. Please discuss a project you supervised.

A. I managed the expansion project at the shopping mall in Greenhaven. It involved increasing the size of the mall by 20 percent. I supervised a staff of fifty-five project team professionals. We completed the project within our budget.

By giving the details of this project, this interviewer demonstrates the type of work of which she's capable.

Never say: "I supervised a mall expansion right outside the city. It went well." This answer is too vague.

Highlighting Your Accomplishments

WHEN YOU GO IN FOR A JOB INTERVIEW, along with learning about your personality and skills, the prospective employer will be very interested in learning about your accomplishments. Your accomplishments give him insight into what you are capable of doing for him and his company. An accomplishment, also known as an achievement, can be defined as something that was successfully completed as a direct result of your efforts.

Listing Your Accomplishments

Prepare a list of your accomplishments prior to your job interview. The accomplishments you choose to highlight should demonstrate your skills and abilities. Remember to use examples of things that came about as a direct result of your efforts. They shouldn't be things that happened to you, like raises or promotions, but rather things you made happen. That's not to say you shouldn't mention that you were promoted as a result of a particular accomplishment, just be sure to explain the accomplishment itself first.

The accomplishments you include on your list should be realistic and verifiable. That's not to say you should be modest on a job interview; go ahead and brag about yourself. However, don't consider stretching the truth—not even just a little. The interviewer may be suspicious of something that sounds too good to be true and if she tries to verify something you told her and cannot, it will certainly reflect poorly on you.

Try to quantify your accomplishments when possible. Use actual numbers or percentages when you are discussing anything that can be expressed in quantifiable terms, such as increases in profits or decreases in costs. Being able to say that you increased sales by 20 percent or cut your department's costs by 35 percent is much better than saying "I increased sales a lot" or "I cut costs greatly."

When deciding which achievements to discuss on an interview, always remember to choose the ones that best demonstrate your ability to do the job you are interviewing for. Highlight skills that you think the prospective employer is looking for in a new employee.

 FACT

Consider keeping a career journal to record all of your achievements and the steps you took to achieve your goals. This will help you be specific on future job interviews. Listing accomplishments as they occur is easier than trying to think back and recall them.

Discussing Your Accomplishments

You will have many opportunities to talk about your accomplishments throughout a job interview. The prospective employer will, of course, ask you direct questions about your accomplishments. You can also impress the interviewer with additional accomplishments if you answer his questions about your skills by not just stating that you have a particular skill, but by discussing what that skill helped you achieve as well.

A prospective employer is likely to ask you questions about your goals, both work-related and personal. Your goals are merely accomplishments waiting to happen. Discuss goals that you have reached or that you are moving toward reaching and talk about the steps you took, or are taking, to do so.

This is your time to brag about what you have done and what

you can do. People are often quite hesitant to speak highly of themselves, thinking that being boastful is obnoxious. This may, in fact, be so in our private lives. However, the job interview is not the time for modesty. You must sell yourself, and to do so you have to show off.

 ALERT!

You may be asked about your personal goals as well as your professional ones. Even when discussing personal goals and achievements, make sure they highlight an ability related to work; for example, perseverance or organizational skills.

Q. Can you tell me about your greatest accomplishment at work?

A. I'm particularly proud of the mentoring program I started about five years ago. I noticed that new employees were having trouble getting acclimated to the company, causing a very high turnover rate during the first year of employment. I developed a program that allowed us to assign each new employee to an employee who had been with the company for at least three years. This allowed new hires to make a smoother transition. Now, 90 percent of new employees are still with us after their one-year anniversaries, up from 50 percent before we started the mentorship program.

The interviewee provides a specific example in response to this question. She also highlights the fact that she took initiative in developing it—she saw a problem and found a solution. She also shows the result of her efforts with actual numbers.

Never say: "I was promoted to assistant director of human resources." While this is wonderful, this interviewee doesn't say what lead to that promotion.

Q. How did you progress at your last job?

A. I was hired as a sales associate by K. R. Nickel Stores seven years ago. I became assistant manager of the girls' clothing department two years later and after two more years was promoted to manager of that department.

This candidate simply describes his ascent up the corporate ladder, giving details, as he was asked to do.

Never say: "I started as a sales associate and seven years later I'm manager of girls' clothing." This interviewee must talk about how he got from point A to point C.

Q. How do you feel about the way your career has pro-gressed so far?

A. I'm pleased with how my career has progressed. When I grad-uated from college, I was hired to work as a trainee at Rogers, Inc., a small advertising agency, which meant I answered the phones and made coffee. I took the initiative and asked for additional work. That gave me the opportunity to prove myself, and I was promoted to assistant account executive after eight months. After two years in that position, during which I worked on several successful ad cam-paigns, I was promoted to account executive. I'm proud of my work there, but it's time for a position with more responsibility.

This candidate takes the time to explain how her career has progressed since her graduation from college. She also makes sure to point out how she contributed to that success.

Never say: "I am very happy with it. I started off answering phones and now look where I am." Don't assume the interviewer knows where you are right now or how you got there.

Q. Why do you think you've been successful in your career so far?

A. I've been successful so far because I've always worked very hard and I've always been willing to accept challenges, usually by seeking them out. I have excellent time management skills that have allowed me to complete projects on time.

This interviewee hasn't relied on luck to achieve success. He has used his skills and motivation to get where he wants to be.

Never say: "I've always been in the right place at the right time." This candidate doesn't seem to think he had anything to do with his own success. If he doesn't believe that, who will?

Q. Which of your accomplishments has given you the most satisfaction?

A. Last year I initiated a program that sent our executives into schools to work with the Young Entrepreneur Program. We sent teams into two area high schools to help the students learn how to run their own businesses. Our executives taught them how to write a business plan, design an ad campaign, make a sales call, and deal with clients. We ended up hiring some of the kids as interns, which worked out really well.

The accomplishment this job candidate has chosen to highlight involves giving back to the community, which is certainly admirable. While it doesn't directly benefit the company in terms of sales or earnings, participation in a program such as the one she describes is good for a company's public image.

Never say: "Finally having a title has been great." This candidate needs to focus on something she did in order to deserve that title.

Q. Do you consider your progress on your current job indicative of your ability?

A. Yes, I do. I was promoted twice on my current job. I was hired as a marketing trainee. After about a year I was promoted to associate account executive, and then after two years I was promoted to account executive. My promotions came about because I proved that I could successfully meet deadlines, win the confidence of clients, and solve problems.

This candidate discusses how and why she was promoted on her job.

Never say: "Yes." This answer lacks specifics.

Q. Describe how you accomplished a work-related goal.

A. When I started working for Daylight Publications, I discovered that I had inherited a huge file cabinet full of photographs. We used photographs in our magazine but usually wound up purchasing stock photos, because our own collection was so disorganized it was impossible to find anything. I designed a filing system and set about putting things in order. I set aside fifteen minutes each day and was able to work my way through the whole collection in about seven months.

This answer demonstrates how the interviewee took the initiative to set a goal in order to save her employer money. She then talks about how she went about reaching that goal by using her organization and time management skills.

Never say: "I wanted to make $50,000 by the time I was twenty-six. I switched jobs a few times and was able to do it." This in no way demonstrates any skills the interviewee has.

Q. Can you describe how you accomplished a personal goal?

A. I wrote a short story and my goal was to get it published. I went to the library and researched which magazines accepted short-story submissions. Then I sent my story to those publications that published stories in the same genre as mine. My story was accepted by one of them and was finally published a little over a year ago.

This candidate talks about the steps he took to reach his personal goal. He used his research skills to find out where to send his story.

Never say: "I won a hot-dog eating contest. I trained for about six months." This answer does not demonstrate any skills that are needed in the workplace.

Q. Tell me how you were of value to your previous employer.

A. My previous employer valued my ability to deal with difficult clients. Whenever we had a client who was very demanding, my boss would ask me to be the one to work with him. She said she knew I was so levelheaded that I would always stay calm, even when a client was really trying my patience.

With this answer the candidate not only says why he thinks his boss values him, he talks about it from her perspective. He presents a skill that will be valuable to this employer as well.

Never say: "I always showed up on time." Showing up on time is expected and doesn't set this candidate apart from any other.

Q. Have you ever had to take over an assignment at the last minute?

A. I've had to do that more than once—actually several times. The most recent was when a colleague was scheduled to attend a meeting out of town and came down with the flu two days before he was supposed to leave. My boss asked me if I could attend the meeting and make the presentation my colleague was supposed to make. I had two days to learn everything about the project. I went over pages and pages of notes and put together a presentation of my own, incorporating input from my colleague, who I spoke to on the phone several times a day.

Not only does this interviewee say he has taken over an assignment at the last minute, he talks about a specific case. He shows how he stepped in and learned what he needed to learn in order to make a successful presentation.

Never say: "Yes, it has happened." He should give an example.

Q. Have you ever received formal recognition for something you accomplished?

A. Yes. I won Salesperson of the Month four times when I was working for Ace Stereo. Those with the largest increase in sales over the previous month were rewarded in this way.

This candidate chose to discuss being rewarded for something that would be valued by any company—high sales volume.

Never say: "I won best dressed at the annual holiday party." Unless this is a candidate for a fashion consulting position, this answer doesn't highlight any skills that will impress the employer.

Q. What has been your greatest accomplishment as part of a team?

A. I worked on a team that developed a program for children who were going home to an empty house after school because their parents worked. We had volunteers who would help the kids with their homework and give them time to just burn off energy after sitting in a classroom all day. By the time we actually opened the center, we had seventy-five children enrolled. That told us we were providing a service that was clearly needed.

This candidate describes in detail the project she considers her greatest accomplishment as part of a team. She talks about what was needed, what they did to fill that need, and what the end result was.

Never say: "I never feel like I accomplish that much on a team." This candidate just admitted she's not a team player— bad idea.

Q. Name the two work-related accomplishments that you are the proudest of.

A. I converted a manual payroll system to a computerized system, which cut down the amount of time we spent on payroll each week. I wrote a manual that explained all bookkeeping department procedures in our company. New employees receive a copy of this manual, which helps them learn their job faster.

Each of the accomplishments this candidate discusses has had a positive result on the company and highlights his many skills.

Never say: "I received a good performance review every year. I was promoted to a supervisory position after just two years." While these are definitely positive things and a reflection of this candidate's ability to do a good job, they really don't address how his accomplishments affected the company.

Q. Tell me about the personal accomplishment that you are the proudest of.

A. Last year I ran a marathon for the first time. I've been a runner for years, but I never ran more than four miles at a time. I began training four months before the big day. It was hard, but I kept going and I ended up finishing in just over four hours, which I've heard is pretty good for a first-time marathoner.

By discussing running a marathon, this candidate demonstrates that she will work hard to reach her goals. She also shows that she is not afraid of a challenge, something her prospective employer should appreciate.

Never say: "I bought my first house." Without an explanation of how she reached this goal, this candidate doesn't show off any strengths with this example.

Q. If I asked your current employer to tell us about your accomplishments, what do you think she would say?

A. She would probably talk about the time she asked me to present a new marketing campaign to one of our more difficult clients. I spent over a week preparing for that presentation. Since I knew this client was hard to please, I had to make sure I anticipated every objection he might have. He actually loved the presentation and the campaign increased sales by 50 percent.

This question gives the candidate a chance to talk about an accomplishment he is proud of. He talks about anticipating possible difficulties and the end result, an increase in sales.

Never say: "I doubt my boss recognized any of my accomplishments. If she did, she certainly didn't tell me." This candidate breaks one of the cardinal rules of job interviewing—never speak negatively about a former boss.

Q. If I asked a college professor about one of your accomplishments, what would he or she say?

A. I worked on a major research project under the supervision of my psychology professor. We collected data over the course of a year and after analyzing the data, we wrote up the results as an article that we submitted to the *Journal of Kangaroo Psychology*. It was accepted and it was published a month before I graduated.

This candidate chose to talk about something that had a tangible result—publication in a professional journal.

Never say: "I got an A in a class that was very difficult." Even though this may have been a great personal achievement for this interviewee, it is probably not something a professor would recognize as a great achievement.

Q. What does success mean to you?

A. I feel I am successful when I do the best job I can possibly do, such as complete a project on time and under budget, and meet or go beyond my own expectations or those of my boss or my client. I also want to achieve the desired result, whether it is to make a profit or reduce a loss for my employer.

This candidate defines success by what he can accomplish for his employer rather than what he can accomplish for himself.

Never say: "Success to me is making a six-figure salary."

Q. Have you ever had to overcome a major obstacle? How did you do it?

A. Yes, I did. My family couldn't afford to pay for college. I applied for as much financial aid as possible, but I still had to work to pay for whatever that didn't cover. I worked after classes every day and on the weekends, too. In the end, in addition to a college degree, I also had some valuable work experience under my belt.

The story this candidate tells demonstrates that she can set a goal—getting a college degree—and reach it through hard work. She even points out that because of her need to overcome this obstacle, she now has valuable work experience.

Never say: "I've been very lucky. I really haven't had any obstacles to overcome." Luck isn't what is going to get this candidate hired. She needs to demonstrate perseverance and therefore should try to find some obstacle to speak about.

Q. What accomplishments have you made so far in reaching your long-range goals?

A. My long-range goal is to be a school principal. I've been teaching for ten years, first at PS 118 and then at PS 114. After five years of teaching second grade at PS 114, I was asked to be grade leader. My experience working with faculty and developing new programs for students has prepared me for the position of assistant principal. I look forward to using my skills to work on some of the projects we discussed earlier.

This candidate has demonstrated how he has taken steps to reach his goal and plans to continue to do so. He also makes a point of talking about the contributions he plans to make in the job that he's interviewing for.

Never say: "I want to be an assistant principal." Since this is the job that he's interviewing for, this answer doesn't show motivation to reach any goals beyond that.

Q. What motivates you to go above and beyond the call of duty?

A. Honestly, I don't have a sense of what is above and beyond the call of duty. It's not like I can just do enough to get by and then stop. When I work on a project, I do my very best, always.

This statement shows that this job candidate is truly a hard worker who cares about her work. It's more than just a job to her. She can't justify giving less than her best effort to any project entrusted to her.

Never say: "Hopefully, if I go above and beyond the call of duty, I'll get recognition for my work." This candidate doesn't seem to be self-motivated since her rewards come from the outside.

Q. What one thing do you think you've done very well on your last job?

A. I think I was very successful in all aspects of my last job. I'm particularly proud of my work with new hires. I developed programs that helped them integrate into the company and this helped our ability to retain them.

Because the interviewer has asked for one thing this person has done well, he is forced to only talk about one thing. He explains why he is particularly proud of that one accomplishment and explains how his success benefited his employer. He also makes a point of saying that this isn't his only success.

Never say: "I can't think of just one thing." If you are asked for one thing, you should be able to come up with something. If not, it appears that you can't think of *anything* you did well at your last job.

Q. What traits will a person need in order to become successful? Do you have these traits?

A. To be successful, a person needs excellent organization and time management skills. She has to get along well with her boss, coworkers, and clients. She must always be willing to learn new skills. Yes, I have all these traits.

This interviewee has chosen some very valuable skills—organization, time management, willingness to learn, and getting along with others.

Never say: "A person must be good at office politics. I've had lots of experience with that, and I'm very good at it." Knowing how to play the game may help you be successful, but your success may not be based on any real skills.

Q. How has your employer rewarded your accomplishments?

A. My employer initially rewarded me by trusting me enough to give me additional responsibility. This gave me a chance to prove myself and I was ultimately rewarded with a big promotion.

This candidate discusses how at first his reward was simply being asked to do more. Did he object to that? No. It only gave him the opportunity to further prove himself so that he received the reward of a promotion.

Never say: "Rewarded? He didn't reward anyone for anything. I guess he thought our paycheck was good enough." This interviewee shouldn't speak with such animosity about his employer.

Q. You seem to have accomplished a lot in your current job. Do you know why you weren't promoted?

A. I wasn't promoted because unfortunately there wasn't a position to promote me to. JFR was a very small family-owned firm. The boss's two sons held the top positions, which were right above my position.

The candidate explains why he couldn't move beyond his current position in spite of his accomplishments. He doesn't seem resentful, but rather accepts this fact.

Never say: "Sure I do. One word—nepotism. The boss's sons hold all the good positions. It doesn't matter how hard you work. You aren't moving up." This candidate is clearly resentful of the way things are at his current job and makes the mistake of letting the interviewer know.

Q. Have you ever come up with new ways to solve a problem?

A. Yes, I have. We had a problem with dismissal from our after-school program. Too many children were leaving at once, causing a bit of chaos in our parking lot. I developed a system for releasing children alphabetically so that parents could pick up siblings in different grades at the same time. If we had released children by grade, parents would have had to wait around for children who were in different grade levels. That would have added to the chaos.

The candidate states a specific problem and then discusses the steps she took to solve it. She even mentions how she anticipated and then prevented a potential problem.

Never say: "I'm lucky. I haven't had to solve any problems." If this candidate hasn't had to solve any problems, how can she be expected to do so in the future?

Q. Have you ever "saved the day" for your employer?

A. Yes, I have. It was the afternoon before our company was hosting a big luncheon. We called the caterer to confirm some of the details, but her number had been disconnected. We found out she had gone out of business and didn't bother to let us know. I called some friends at other companies and got a list of caterers together, called them, and got someone to do the job. My boss couldn't believe I managed to hire someone on such short notice.

The interviewee, by giving this example, shows how her resourcefulness helped her solve her employer's problem.

Never say: "I've saved many days for them. I always have to fix everyone else's mistakes." This answer, even if it is true, makes the interviewee appear arrogant.

Q. Have you ever been asked to take on a project because of your unique skill or ability?

A. Our senior developer regularly asks me to troubleshoot new programs. I've been very successful at figuring out why programs aren't working properly and I can usually do it pretty quickly, allowing the team to move forward.

This candidate chose to talk about a skill that will be as valuable to his prospective employer as it is to his current one.

Never say: "I'm very good at planning parties, so when my boss's secretary was retiring he asked me to plan the party." This skill probably won't be very important to the prospective employer.

Q. Have you ever done something that directly helped your employer either increase profits or decrease costs?

A. I recently found a way to help my employer save money on office supplies. For years, they bought office supplies from the same place. It was several blocks away, so it was pretty convenient. I have found that shopping online is almost always less expensive than shopping in a store, so I did a little comparison shopping and I found an online source for our office supplies at a savings of 40 percent from what we were paying for the same items. Plus, the items are delivered, which is even more convenient. As long as we order several items at once, delivery is free.

This interviewee's answer illustrates how she looks out for her employer's best interests.

Never say: "I just go about doing my job. I guess that increases their profits, doesn't it?" This candidate needs to remember she's trying to sell herself to this employer. Instead of saying she'll "just do the job," she needs to show why she'd be great at it.

Q. **Have you ever been assigned a project you didn't think you'd be able to get through? If so, what happened?**

A. I've been assigned many projects that seemed difficult at first, but I refuse to think of any project as impossible. Before I begin any project, I think about how I'm going to tackle it. I come up with a plan and take it step by step. If I think I need help with a project, I ask for advice from those with more experience.

This candidate demonstrates that she will not be defeated by any project. Yet she is not averse to asking for help when she needs it. She explains how she approaches all projects in a systematic fashion.

Never say: "There isn't a project I can't get through." There's a difference between self-assurance and cockiness. Without explaining what she does in order to get through difficult projects, she just sounds cocky.

Q. **Is there anything I've missed?**

A. Well, I did want to mention that I was honored by my organization's board of directors for developing a program that reached out to a large number of senior citizens in need of financial assistance. We now help just over 650 seniors each year.

The candidate uses this opportunity to bring to the interviewer's attention an accomplishment she didn't discuss previously.

Never say: "No. I think you just about covered it all. Are we done?"

CHAPTER 6

Questions about Your Education

WHEN PROSPECTIVE EMPLOYERS INTERVIEW recent graduates without much experience, they can learn a lot about applicants by asking questions about their school experience. Therefore, if you're interviewing for jobs straight out of school, you should be prepared to answer a lot of questions about your education. Even if you've been working for a few years, you may still be asked about your education, so it's important to have your answers ready.

How You Spent Your College Years

The interviewer will want to know about your performance as a student. As you know, grades don't always tell the whole story. A failing grade may mean more than an inability in a particular subject and a high grade may mean more than great achievement.

The interviewer will want to know how you felt about particular subjects, which ones you found challenging, and which ones you thought were a piece of cake. She may ask which teachers you liked and why. All of this information lets her get a better look at who you are.

In addition to simple questions like "Where did you go to school?" and "What was your major?" the interviewer will likely ask you about activities you participated in outside the classroom. She will want to know about your extracurricular activities like membership in on-campus clubs and organizations, work on student-run publications, and community service. All these activities contributed to your education and are included in what you will bring to an employer. Think about your activities in terms of the skills they helped you develop. When you can't prove your worth by talking about your work experience, you must prove it by discussing what you did during your time in school.

 ESSENTIAL

When asked about extracurricular activities, you should think of each one as a job. What contributions did you make? Can you quantify them? Did you help raise money for a charity? How much? Did you work for your school newspaper? How many hours a week did that involve? What were your successes and what were your failures?

Many students gain work experience by doing an internship. If you did an internship, be prepared to discuss that experience in detail. The interviewer will want to know what you learned there and what contributions you made.

The prospective employer has something else on her agenda, too. She is interested in knowing why and how you made the choices you've made. For example, she wants to know how you chose your college. She wants to find out how you decided on your major. Seeing how you made these very important choices offers her the opportunity to see what process you go through when making a decision. If your current career choice is different from what you studied in college, you should be ready to discuss how your major prepared you for your occupation even though the two aren't directly related.

Q. I see you majored in English. Are you prepared for a job in marketing and sales?

A. As an English major I had to do a large amount of reading and needed to retain all of it. Reading and absorbing the literature on the products I'll be selling will be a snap. I believe college also prepared me to manage my time well. I do have hands-on experience in this field as well; I worked in various sales positions in order to put myself through school.

Notice that the interviewee doesn't make any excuses for working in a field outside his major. Instead, he talks about how his major qualifies him for this job. He also talks about the fact that he has sales experience.

Never say: "I think I'll have an easier time finding a job in my field, but the one you advertised sounds good, too." This answer doesn't show how his skills transfer to this new discipline.

Q. Why did you choose Adams University?

A. Adams University has an accredited business school. It is ranked third in the nation. The university also has a great cross-country team and I wanted to try out for it.

This candidate put a lot of thought into choosing a college, implying that's how she makes all her decisions. She also uses this opportunity to brag about the quality of her education.

Never say: "My best friend was going there." This applicant doesn't demonstrate that she puts a lot of thought into important decisions.

Q. I see you majored in marketing. What courses did you take outside your major?

A. I took a few psych classes because I felt that knowing how people think would be to my advantage in marketing. I took a some art classes because I really enjoy that. I also took writing courses, because I thought that was an important skill to have.

Instead of just giving a list of courses, this candidate talks about why she took them. She even explains how two of the subjects will help in her career.

Never say: "I decided just to take extra courses in my major." While this candidate may think she's showing how much she knows about her field, having taken extra courses in it, she is actually showing that she's not well rounded.

Q. Did you have any teachers who influenced you?

A. Yes, I did. It goes all the way back to junior high school. Mr. Danzer was my earth science teacher. He loved the subject and he loved teaching. I think both these things came across in his ability to teach. It showed me that if a person loves what he does, he's more likely to excel at it. That was good to know when it came time to choose a career.

This candidate tells which teacher influenced him and how.

Never say: "No." If you can't think of one single teacher, perhaps you can mention the qualities of several who had some sort of impact on you.

Q. Why did you choose to major in philosophy?

A. From a very early age I wanted to be a lawyer. When I started to do my research, I found out that undergraduates who want to go to law school should take a lot of liberal arts classes. During my freshman year, I took different courses in the school of liberal arts and sciences and I liked philosophy the best, so I decided to make it my concentration.

This applicant shows that she made an informed choice when choosing her major.

Never say: "It looked interesting." While you should choose a major you think is interesting, that shouldn't be your only criteria.

Q. What did you gain from attending college?

A. I gained knowledge about this field. I was able to use what I learned in class on the internship I did last summer at the *Tallahassee Tribune.* College is where I learned to be independent. There wasn't anyone pushing me to complete assignments on time, so I had to learn how to manage my time well and stay organized.

This candidate talks about things he learned both in and out of the classroom. He includes technical skills as well as soft skills—time management and organization.

Never say: "I got my degree." Isn't that on the resume? The candidate needs to come up with more than this.

Q. What was your favorite subject in high school? What was your favorite subject in college?

A. English was my favorite subject in high school. I did a lot of writing in English. I liked working hard to put together a paper and then getting feedback in the form of a grade. My favorite classes in college were those in my major. I actually took only one marketing class before I declared marketing as my major. I found the subject matter so interesting that I started looking into it as a career choice.

This candidate explains why English was her favorite subject and in the process demonstrates her skill as a writer, which she knows will be an important part of her job. By stating that her major was her favorite subject in college, she shows that she is dedicated to the field.

Never say: "In high school I liked social studies. My favorite subject in college was sociology." This candidate needs to explain why these two subjects were her favorites.

Ⓔ ALERT!

> If you are asked on an interview what your least favorite class was, try to stay as far away as possible from anything you will use in your career. Don't bring up failing a class unless you are asked a direct question about that.

Q. What were your least favorite subjects in high school and college?

A. My least favorite subject in high school was home economics. I helped with the housekeeping at home—I didn't want to have to deal with it at school, too. I liked most of the classes I took in college. If I had to pick my least favorite I guess it would have to be biology. We had to dissect a fetal pig, and I had a problem doing that.

The candidate picked classes unrelated to the job he's applying for. Notice also that he didn't say he disliked the classes because of their difficulty.

Never say: "My least favorite classes were geometry and matrix algebra. I couldn't get it. I guess math isn't my strong suit." This candidate makes the mistake of volunteering information about his weaknesses. While they may not be related to this job, they are challenges that defeated him.

Q. What extracurricular activities did you participate in?

A. During my junior year of college, I was president of the psychology club. Then in my senior year I was editor of the yearbook. I wrote for both my high school and college newspapers, too.

This candidate highlights his leadership experience. He also calls attention to a very important skill—writing.

Never say: "Academics took up all my time. I didn't have much time for anything else." This candidate may think she's showing what a dedicated student she was, but extracurricular activities enhance one's college experience. She should try to think of some valuable experience she had outside the classroom.

Q. I see it took you four and a half years to graduate. Can you explain that?

A. I had a difficult time adjusting during my freshman year. I wasn't quite ready for all the demands of college. I had to take a few classes over. During the summer between my freshman and sophomore years, I went to a few workshops to help me improve my study skills and my time management skills. By the time I was a sophomore, I was a much more serious student.

This candidate doesn't make excuses for his failings, but rather speaks about how he overcame them and how he succeeded in the end.

Never say: "I had these really tough professors my freshman year. They wouldn't cut me any slack. When you're a freshman, you get stuck with teachers no one else wants." This candidate only wants to blame everyone else for his failure.

Q. Aside from coursework, what was the most enriching part of your college education?

A. I was very involved on the programming committee. As a matter of fact, I was chair during my senior year. We were responsible for planning on-campus events for the student body. The goal was to hold events that were well attended and safe. That meant hiring entertainment that appealed to the majority of students and making sure campus security was present to enforce the rules.

This applicant talks about her work on this committee as if it were a job. She explains her goals and how she met them.

Never say: "I was in some campus clubs and that was fun." This applicant needs to do a better job of explaining what those clubs were and what her responsibilities were.

Q. I see you had an internship in this field. What did you learn from it?

A. My internship at Carlson Corporate allowed me to get some hands-on experience in this field that I wouldn't have gotten in classes alone. I learned that jobs in this field are often stressful and long hours are often required. On the other hand, I got to find out how wonderful it is when you're on a team that helps land a big account as a result of hard work.

This applicant speaks about what he gained from the internship and what he learned about the positive and negative aspects of working in the field.

Never say: "Not a heck of a lot. I was just a glorified gopher." Even if all he did was deliver mail and make copies, this candidate should be able to come up with something he learned just from being exposed to the work environment of this particular field.

Q. Why haven't you done any internships?

A. I would have loved to have done an internship, but unfortunately I had to work my way through college. Most internships don't pay that well. However, as you can see from my resume, I made a point of finding work within this industry. Even though I was in the mailroom, I was still exposed to the field.

While internships are important, sometimes extenuating circumstances get in the way. This candidate has no choice but to be honest about that. However, she explains how she tried to make up for not being able to do an internship.

Never say: "I won't work for free." This candidate sounds like she's only concerned with money and experience is worth nothing to her.

Q. How did you spend your summers during college?

A. I worked every summer to earn money for books and part of my tuition. I had this great job at a day camp. I started off as a counselor the summer before my senior year of high school, moved up to group leader the summer after I graduated, and then became assistant director.

This applicant takes the opportunity to show off a little. He stayed at the same job for several years and was promoted to a supervisory position.

Never say: "I rested. School's hard." If school is hard, wait until you try work. And you don't get over two months off each year.

Ⓔ ESSENTIAL

How you spent your summers while in school says a lot about you. Your experience may not be career-related, but it may give you the opportunity to highlight some positive qualities about yourself. If you were asked back to the same job summer after summer, your prospective employer can assume you were a good worker.

Q. What grade did you receive in your favorite class?

A. My favorite class was intro to journalism. It was actually pretty tough at first. Everything I handed in came back marked up in red ink. I must have gotten D's on the first four assignments. There were a few times that I found just the right words to capture an event, though, and I loved that feeling, so I stuck with it. Fortunately my professor gave us the opportunity to redo our work for a higher grade, and although it took some extra work, ultimately I got an A in the class.

It's easy to like a class if you don't have to work hard for a good grade. This applicant explains why journalism was her favorite class despite having to work hard.

Never say: "Intro to journalism. I got an A." Without saying more than that, the interviewer is left to wonder whether the candidate liked that class simply because she got an A in it.

Q. What grade did you receive in your least favorite class?

A. My least favorite class was art history. I know other people who took the class with other professors, got a C, and loved it. I hated the class and got an A. I didn't learn anything. I just had to show up for every class.

Clearly this candidate likes to work hard and isn't impressed with getting rewarded for "just showing up."

Never say: "I got a D in it. It was organic chemistry, the hardest class I ever took. I can't believe how much I studied and all I ended up with was a D." Other than getting a bad grade, this candidate doesn't explain why this was his least favorite class. He just sounds like a sore loser.

Q. Why did you decide to major in elementary education?

A. When I was in high school, I took an assessment test to help me figure out what career I should go into. When I got my results, teaching was one of the occupations on the list, along with several others like psychology, social work, and nursing. When I started researching the occupations in more detail, I discovered that teaching was the one that appealed to me most.

This candidate put a lot of thought into choosing an occupation. This answer not only shows her dedication to teaching but also that she makes decisions carefully.

Never say: "I like children." While it's important to like children if you want to teach them, liking children doesn't necessarily mean you'll be good at teaching.

Q. I see you transferred to Hamford University from Sannau County Community College. Why did you start at a two-year school?

A. I knew I wanted to earn a bachelor's degree. I also wanted to go to Hamford, but the cost of a four-year education there was extremely high. I decided to take my core classes at a community college to save money. I first checked to make sure Hamford would take my credits. Since Sannau is a very well respected community college, I knew I would get a decent education there.

By giving this answer, the interviewee demonstrates that she is a very practical person. She spends money wisely but doesn't compromise her goals. She also doesn't do something without first investigating it.

Never say: "I thought Sannau would be a good place to start my education." This doesn't explain what led to the transfer.

Q. What would your professors say about you?

A. My professors would say I always turned in high-quality work. They would say I contributed to classroom discussions by offering interesting comments and asking good questions. They would also say I was willing to help other students.

This candidate takes the opportunity to highlight some positive attributes.

Never say: "They liked me." This interviewee needs to explain why they liked her.

Q. What courses best prepared you for this job?

A. I took a course in research and bibliographic methods that provided me with the technical skills to do this job. The most important thing I learned in that class was that there is a resource available to answer almost all questions. I also took several classes in children's and young adult literature. I saw from the job description that the person who takes this position will also have to spend several hours a week in the children's department.

This candidate not only lists some courses he took, but also explains how they will help him do the job should he be hired.

Never say: "I took research and bibliographic methods and some children's lit classes. I think they'll be helpful." This candidate tells what classes he took but isn't specific about how they will enable him to do his job.

Q. Are you planning to get your MBA?

A. I would like to do that. I'm trying to find a program with a schedule that won't interfere with work.

❦

This interviewee knows that an MBA is highly valued in her field, but she anticipates that her potential employer might be concerned that her work schedule would be compromised if she pursues one. She heads off those fears.

Never say: "I've already been accepted at NJU. The classes start at 5:45, so I'm hoping it will be okay if I cut out of here early three days a week." If the employer had a choice between this candidate and one who wouldn't need his schedule adjusted, who do you think she would choose? In addition, any discussion of that sort can wait until a job offer is received.

Q. What elective accounting courses did you take?

A. I took three auditing classes because I knew I wanted to work in public accounting. I also took an international accounting class. In this global economy I knew that would come in handy at some point in my career.

❦

This candidate explains how she chose courses she would be able to use professionally.

Never say: "I took a taxation class, an auditing class, and a corporate accounting class that all fit nicely into my schedule." This answer doesn't show that the candidate selected classes that would benefit her in her career.

Q. Have you ever had a disagreement with a professor? How did you handle it?

A. I disagreed about a grade I received once. I spent a lot of time researching and writing a paper for a history class. When I got the paper back with a B, I was very disappointed. After thinking about it for a day, I decided to talk to the professor. He asked me what grade I thought I deserved. I said I thought I had earned an A on the paper and explained why. He said he would read the paper over and regrade it if he found my arguments were valid. The next day he told me he changed my grade to an A.

This student knows how to stand up for herself when there is something she feels strongly about. She demonstrates how she persuaded her teacher to change her grade by presenting her arguments in a calm manner after waiting a day to collect her thoughts.

Never say: "I was very unhappy about a grade a professor gave me, but I didn't bother saying anything about it."

Q. What was the most difficult assignment you had while in school?

A. I took a creative writing class. It was one of several electives I could choose from outside my major. I had to write a poem. I discovered I'm not really good at that sort of thing.

This interviewee chose to discuss an assignment that was entirely unrelated to his major and to anything he would be expected to do at this job.

Never say: "I hated writing papers, so any assignment that involved doing that was difficult." Since some writing is generally required at all jobs, this probably was not the best choice.

Q. Your GPA wasn't very high. Can you please explain that?

A. During my first two years of college, I was kind of immature and didn't work hard enough. I worked really hard my junior and senior years, but unfortunately those first two years really brought down my GPA. It was hard to recover from that.

This candidate acknowledges that he was responsible for his low GPA, but also talks about how he worked hard to raise it.

 Never say: "Just bad luck, I guess."

Ⓔ QUESTION?

How should I explain poor grades?
You should take full responsibility for your grades, even if they aren't good. Don't place the blame on anyone else. Keep your answer positive by talking about what you did to improve.

Q. What was your favorite thing about high school?

A. My favorite thing about high school was working on the school newspaper. I was the managing director my senior year. I learned how to manage deadlines and I helped our editors organize projects they were working on.

The interviewee picked something that allowed her to show two of her skills—time management and organization. She knows that employers in her field value these skills.

Never say: "I loved everything about high school." While the interviewer may appreciate the candidate's positive attitude, this answer doesn't tell her anything about him.

Q. What did you like most about college?

A. I really enjoyed playing on the volleyball team. During my freshman and sophomore years the team wasn't as strong as it could have been. We pulled together and worked very hard, and by my junior year we were ranked number two in our division. By my senior year we were ranked first place.

This candidate's mention of her participation on an athletic team draws attention to her ability to work on a team. From her research, she knows employees of this company often work on teams.

Never say: "I loved my classes." While that is admirable, this candidate doesn't say why this is so. If his classes were truly his favorite part of college, he needs to explain how something he did contributed to that feeling.

Q. Why did you choose to go away to college rather than going to one near your home?

A. I wanted to be responsible for myself, and I knew that wouldn't happen at home. By living in the dorms, I had no choice but to manage my own time, budget my money, and set my own limits.

This candidate saw going away to college as a learning experience, both in and out of the classroom.

Never say: "My parents didn't like the guy I was dating, so they sent me away to school." Have you ever heard of giving too much information?

THE EVERYTHING PRACTICE INTERVIEW BOOK

Q. Why didn't you go to college?

A. I didn't know what I wanted to do at the time and I didn't want to waste my parents' money. I thought I would gain more from working than I would from school. Now that I have work experience, and I know I want to stay in this field, I plan to get my degree. The city university has a program that accommodates working adults.

The interviewees decision to postpone college, as she explains it, was a clearly thought-out one. While she indicates her intention to continue her education, she is also quick to point out that it won't affect her work schedule.

Never say: "I don't know. I didn't really give it much thought." Not giving a lot of thought to such an important decision doesn't say much about this applicant, or maybe it says too much.

Q. Why didn't you finish college?

A. I left school because of financial reasons. My parents couldn't afford my tuition, so I decided to work for a few years. The experience was actually a great one for me. I learned a lot from it. I'm planning to take some classes next semester. I just heard about a great program that offers classes online. I even checked the program out with the State Education Department and it's legitimate.

Dropping out of school for financial reasons is certainly acceptable. This candidate speaks positively of her work experience, claiming that she gained something from it. Her plan to take some classes won't affect her work schedule.

Never say: "I didn't really like school that much." A candidate who drops out when she's not having fun is probably not going to be the first one hired.

CHAPTER 7

Discussing Your Work History

WHILE EXPERIENCE ISN'T EVERYTHING, it does count for a lot when a prospective employer must decide whether you are the most qualified candidate for the job. What you have done on your past jobs is very meaningful and an interviewer will spend a lot of time learning about your work history so he can discover how it will affect your future performance. That is why it is so important that you take great care to present your past well.

How to Present Your Past

What does it mean to "present your past well?" After years of spending many of your waking hours working, here's a chance to let your past jobs work for you. Answering questions about your work history gives you the opportunity to highlight things you want to call to a prospective employer's attention. You also want to downplay things you would rather not have her focus on. You want to tell your side of the story, in your own words, and in greater depth than you could ever do on a resume.

When prospective employers ask questions about your work history, they want to know more than where you worked, how long you worked there, and what your job duties were. They can learn that from your resume. They would love to hear about the skills you gained at each of your previous jobs, but that information is probably on your resume as well. Now it's time to get beyond the resume and learn more about you than they ever could from a one- or two-page document. Employers want to know not only what skills you picked up on your prior jobs, but how you used those skills. They want to know what you liked about each job, and what you didn't like. They want to find out if you got along with your boss. Employers want to know why you left each of your jobs, or why you stayed. They want to know what motivates you. They want to know how your career has progressed and how you expect it to progress in the future. And most importantly, employers want to know what you can bring to them as an employee.

ESSENTIAL

Use your resume as a guide when you prepare to answer questions about your work history. As you look at each job you have listed on your resume, try to recall specific details about it. Why did you take that job? Why did you eventually leave it? What were your job duties? Sometimes it's difficult to remember how long you were at each job, never mind what you did there. A little time spent preparing in advance can help save you from some awkward moments of silence during an interview as you try to answer a prospective employer's questions.

When answering questions about your work history, make every answer count. Each answer should tell the interviewer how your experience qualifies you for this job. You should give specific examples drawn from your experiences. When an interviewer asks if you've ever performed a particular activity on a past job, he generally expects more than a yes or no answer. As with every type of question so far, your answer needs to give details.

Q. What was your first job?

A. My very first job was in a deli. I worked there every summer from ninth grade until I graduated from college. At first I was hired to do odd jobs, but once I was old enough, I worked behind the counter, serving customers. I was the youngest employee there but my boss always said I was the hardest-working one.

Although this job was unrelated to his career, his longevity there, as well as his former boss's opinion of him, lets the interviewer know that he was a valuable employee.

Never say: "It was in a deli." This candidate needs to give more details about his job.

Q. Out of the jobs you've had, which was your favorite?

A. My favorite job was teaching at the Wee Ones Preschool. I like my current job at Parkside Elementary, but I realize now that I prefer to work with preschoolers. That's why I want to work here.

This candidate has chosen a job that is related to the one that she is being interviewed for.

Never say: "I loved working at Sam's Steakhouse in college. The other waitresses and I had so much fun together." Not only does this candidate choose a job unrelated to her chosen field, she doesn't sound very serious about working at all.

Q. Tell me about your current job.

A. I am a junior architect at James, Jones, and Johnson. I work on the commercial building division. As part of a team of five architects, I help design shopping centers and office complexes.

The interviewee describes his current job, as he is asked to do. He discusses his work as part of a team because he knows that this prospective employer also utilizes a team structure.

Never say: "I work at James, Jones, and Johnson. It's right there on my resume." The interviewer wants the candidate to describe the job in his own words.

Q. Tell me about a typical day at work.

A. Every day is different. The one constant is that I spend from two to three hours working at the reference desk each day, assisting patrons. That leaves either four or five hours to tend to what I refer to as "behind the scenes" work. I'm in charge of library publicity, so I might have to write and send out press releases or update our mailing list. If it's the middle of the month, I'll be working on the monthly newsletter. When I'm not working on publicity, I'm selecting books to order, or weeding outdated material from our collection.

The candidate takes this opportunity to discuss her many responsibilities.

Never say: "Every day is different. I do so many things, it's hard to say what a typical day is." This person is busy, but doing what?

Q. What do you like about your job?

A. I like it when I can successfully resolve a customer's problem. If the customer walks away satisfied, I'm happy.

This candidate, by giving this answer, shows what motivates her—keeping customers happy.

Never say: "My boss is nice." This candidate should have chosen something about her job that provides satisfaction.

Ⓔ ESSENTIAL

When you are asked to discuss something you like about your job, you should talk about something that is related to what you do for the company.

Q. What kinds of jobs did you have during college?

A. I had a variety of jobs while I was going to college and since I was paying my own way, I sometimes had more than one job. I worked as a waiter, a door-to-door salesman, and a data entry clerk. I learned a lot about interacting tactfully with different people, and I also developed my office and computer skills.

In addition to demonstrating how industrious he is (working his way through school), this candidate shows how he developed skills in different areas through his experience.

Never say: "I just had some menial jobs." No matter how menial he thought those jobs were, he should have taken the time to figure out what skills they helped him develop.

Q. Describe your favorite boss.

A. That would have to be my boss at Triangle Optical. Paul was the most demanding boss I've ever had. He expected so much from our department. What set him apart from other supervisors was that he worked tirelessly alongside us—he was just as demanding of himself. He always gave everyone the credit they deserved.

By telling his prospective employer what traits he valued in a former boss, this applicant is letting him know what he will be like as a supervisor.

Never say: "I like a boss who is flexible and fair." This candidate should give a specific example.

Q. Describe your least favorite boss.

A. I'd rather not mention names since this industry is so small. I had a boss who never planned anything in advance. We were always racing to meet deadlines, running out of supplies, or finding ourselves short staffed because he couldn't say no to anyone who asked for a day off.

While it's best not to say something negative about a former employer, the interviewee must answer the question. She is somewhat restrained in her criticism, though. All this candidate says is that she prefers someone who is more structured. Rejecting her former boss's management style implies that this is not what she'd be like as a manager. She also uses discretion by refusing to reveal who her boss was.

Never say: "His name was Joe Josephson and he was my boss at BRK Audio. He was too demanding." This applicant doesn't hesitate to reveal her boss's name and doesn't give enough of a reason for choosing him as her worst boss.

Q. You seem to be climbing the corporate ladder in your current job. Why leave now?

A. I'm choosing to leave now because my goals have changed. I want to use my public relations skills at a nonprofit organization such as this one.

This applicant is making a change to another industry, but shows how he can still utilize his skills to meet his new goals.

Never say: "My bosses are crazy. I can't stay there anymore." Remember that making negative comments about any employer is a bad idea.

Q. I see three jobs listed on your resume. Can you tell me what you learned from each of them?

A. I learned a lot on each of my jobs, so it's hard to pick one thing from each, but I'll try. When I worked in customer support at CSV, I learned how to help our software users troubleshoot problems. When I worked as a software trainer at Circle Tech, I learned that I needed to find a common ground when teaching a large group of people, because not everyone has the same level of skills. I learned to manage employees at my job as assistant to the head of training at APCO.

Knowing about the job that he's applying for helped the applicant answer this question. He has picked one skill from each job that will be required for the job with this employer.

Never say: "I learned to be at work on time from my first job. Then from my second job, I learned to keep my mouth shut. . . ." This applicant hasn't chosen to talk about skills that will be required by his prospective employer.

Q. Do you find your job rewarding?

A. I found my job very rewarding for a long time. It hasn't been as rewarding lately. While I love my new responsibilities, I miss working with clients. That is what attracted me to this position—the combination of supervisory responsibilities and client contact.

It's okay for the interviewee to say she doesn't find her current job rewarding. She explains why she feels this way without placing blame anywhere. With this answer, she also shows that she knows about the position she's interviewing for and explains why she is better suited for it.

Never say: "No, I don't. They took away everything I liked about my job." This candidate sounds very angry.

Q. What about your current job isn't very rewarding?

A. I think every job has something about it that isn't rewarding. There is a lot of paperwork and I don't find that particularly rewarding, but I know it needs to be done.

This candidate understands the reality of work. Some job duties are rewarding, while others are not. She chose something that many people don't find particularly rewarding—paperwork.

Never say: "Everything about it is rewarding." The interviewer will question this applicant's sincerity. If he finds everything about his job rewarding, he would have no reason to leave.

Q. How have your other jobs prepared you for the one at this company?

A. I've worked on the retail end of the office supplies industry for the past ten years. I know what customers want and in turn what the retail outlets want. I know the industry and I know the products. That is what qualifies me to be a sales rep for Roxy Staple Company.

This candidate is confident of his abilities and that comes across in his response.

Never say: "I learned a lot on my previous jobs. My skills qualify me for a job with your company." Which skills would those be?

Q. Your last job was very different than the ones you had before. Why did you take that job?

A. I was thinking of going back to school to be a veterinarian. I mentioned this to my neighbor, a vet, and he offered me a job in his office. I love animals, but before I made the commitment to go to veterinary school, I wanted to make sure I'd be happy working with them and especially dealing with sick ones. It turned out that wasn't right for me after all.

This candidate has a good explanation for why she took a job that has nothing at all to do with her current career path. In doing so she also shows off her decision-making skills.

Never say: "The job was available and they wanted to hire me." This candidate had no particular reason for taking a job outside her field, leading the potential employer to question her goals.

Q. How do you feel about the way your department was managed on your last job?

A. I think it was managed effectively.

This isn't a glowing review, but the candidate didn't say anything negative, either. Even if he thinks his manager was a bumbling fool, he avoids saying so. Badmouthing his boss would make the applicant look bad.

Never say: "The manager was awful."

Q. You've never worked in widget manufacturing before. How have your jobs in the publishing industry prepared you for this?

A. Taking a product, whether it's a widget or a book, from its inception to the hands of the consumer takes a lot of planning. You have to put together a budget and set deadlines. You need to make sure your current staff can handle the work and hire consultants if necessary. You may even have to handle crises along the way, should problems arise. I dealt with such things on a daily basis while working in publishing, and would be able to use the same planning and management skills to help your company.

By focusing on his job responsibilities and talking about them in general terms, this candidate is able to show how he can transfer his skills from one industry to another.

Never say: "I had to work long hours in publishing and I know people in your industry work long hours, too." This doesn't tell the interviewer anything about the candidate or his skills.

Q. How would your previous supervisor describe you?

A. Ms. Roberts respects me. She would describe me as a diligent worker who takes great care to do an excellent job on every project she assigns me. I complete all work on time. She appreciates the fact that I am very friendly and usually asks me to be our department's "welcome wagon" when a new employee starts.

A little bit of bragging is a good thing. This applicant knows that to answer with anything less than this amount of confidence might lead the interviewer to think he's unsure of himself.

Never say: "I've worked there for three years and she's never complained." Saying your boss never complained about you doesn't exactly shout "great employee!"

Q. What decisions have you had to make on your current job?

A. When I planned career workshops for students, I had to decide what topics to feature, when to hold the workshops, and who would speak at them. I had to decide what software to purchase for our public computers, within the constraints of our budget. I also made decisions about hiring and firing student aides.

By giving specific examples, this candidate highlights her skills in planning events, making purchasing decisions, working within a budget, and making personnel decisions.

Never say: "I didn't really get to make too many decisions." This applicant should have realized that the interviewer was asking this question because decision-making is required on the job she's interviewing for. She should have taken a moment to think of one or two decisions she made. Even if they didn't seem significant, it would have been better than not giving an answer.

Q. What were the reasons you went to work for your two prior employers?

A. I went to work for Pear Computers right out of college. They had an excellent one-year training program, and I knew I would learn a lot there. After I completed the training program, I stayed there for three years. I went to work for my next employer, Bell Technology, because they offered me a position with greater responsibilities than Pear Computers could.

This candidate took advantage of the opportunity to partic-ipate in a training program where he could add to what he learned in school. After taking part in the training program, he stayed at the company for a while, implying that he didn't just take the training and run. His next job was clearly a step up.

Never say: "Each of my last two employers offered a good salary and benefits." More thought should go into choosing to go to work for someone.

Q. Why did you leave your last job?

A. I left my last job because I knew the industry was facing an uncertain future. I researched this industry, saw the growth poten-tial, and knew I could make a significant contribution.

This job candidate plans for the future. He doesn't make rash decisions; he does his homework first.

Never say: "I was bored." Without further explanation, this isn't a good enough reason to leave your job.

Q. You've been at your job for several years. What makes you want to leave?

A. I've completed what I set out to do. When I first started working there, the company was just getting started. They needed someone who had the skills to help them grow. They are very successful now and I feel like I've completed my mission. I know I could better use my skills in a growing company such as yours.

Not only does this applicant show off her accomplishments at her current job, she tells her potential employer what she can do for his company.

Never say: "I want to make more money." This may be part of it, but it isn't a good enough reason to give to a prospective employer.

Q. How is your present job different from the ones you had before it?

A. As a senior accounting clerk, I supervise three payroll clerks and a bookkeeper. This is the first time I've had to supervise other people.

This applicant talks about how she has increased responsibilities at her job.

Never say: "I have to use a computer now and I also have to work late." Neither of these things illustrates the candidate's growth.

Q. What duties of your last job did you find difficult?

A. I found it difficult to fire people. Even though I always put a lot of thought into deciding whether or not to terminate someone, I knew I was affecting someone's livelihood.

No one could fault someone for disliking this unpleasant duty.

Never say: "Dealing with my boss every day." Oops.

Q. Describe how your career progressed over the last five years. Was it aligned with the goals you set for yourself?

A. When I graduated from the community college, I knew I wanted to work as a store manager. I also knew I would have to work my way up, so I took a job as a sales associate at Dress Corral. After a lot of hard work I was promoted to assistant department manager after two years. After being in that job for a year, I got a job as manager of the ladies' accessories department at P. J. Coopers, and I've been there for the last two years. With my experience, I'm ready for the next step—store manager.

This job candidate shows exactly how her career has progressed and how she is now ready for a job with this employer.

Never say: "I really didn't set any goals. I took the sales associate job because it was the only place that wanted someone with my skills. It's been nice to be able to move up." It's okay if this candidate didn't have a plan to start with, but she should have made one along the way. It seems she's let others set goals for her. If she doesn't have a plan, this prospective employer can't predict what she'll do next.

Q. How would those who worked under you describe you as a supervisor?

A. My staff at AQA Associates knew I was someone who worked hard and expected the same of them. They also felt I was fair, never asking them to do something I wasn't willing to do myself. My office door was always open and they felt they could come to me to discuss any problem they might have.

This applicant describes the qualities of a good supervisor. Not only does she tell the interviewer how her staff felt about her, she tells them why they felt that way. Notice how sure she is of her answer, never saying, "I think they felt this way." She knows exactly how she is regarded as a supervisor.

Never say: "I think they thought I did a good job."

Q. This job carries with it much more responsibility than you've had before. Are you ready?

A. I am definitely ready. I've been working as assistant registrar for five years. I have learned a lot at Burberry College. I've worked very closely with my boss and I know what her job entails. She is also confident in my ability to move on.

This candidate restates his experience and shares with the interviewer the vote of confidence his boss gave him.

Never say: "Sure. Why not? I've paid my dues."

Q. Have you had to do any traveling for work?

A. I've had to do some traveling for my job. I went to Asia several times. I enjoy traveling and hope to do more of it on this job. I find it helpful to have face-to-face meetings with clients periodically rather than doing everything through conference calls.

This applicant knows that his potential employer requires extensive traveling and although he hasn't done a lot of it, he makes sure to point out that it's something he wants to do more of.

Never say: "They had me traveling all over the place." This candidate doesn't sound very enthusiastic.

Q. What do you think this job offers that your last job did not?

A. This job offers me the opportunity to use my research skills. I have mostly administrative duties on my current job, with some research duties. I look forward to a job that is primarily research oriented with some administrative duties.

This applicant has both administrative and research skills, as she points out to the interviewer. She wants to use them in a different way than she does on her current job.

Never say: "This job offers me the opportunity to do research. I always wanted to do that." There's nothing to indicate that this person has any research skills. If there are many candidates to choose from, the employer may not be willing to hire someone who still requires training.

Q. What kind of person do you find it difficult to work with? What kind of person do you find it easy to work with?

A. I find it difficult to work with someone who does sloppy work, takes credit when he hasn't earned it, or who tries to get away with doing as little as possible. I find it easy to work with someone who is ambitious, takes the time to do the best job possible, and does more than is asked of her.

"That's not me" is what the interviewee is really saying when she reveals which traits she doesn't like in a coworker. Ambitious, does the best job possible—"now, that's me," the job candidate is saying.

Never say: "I don't like working with someone who isn't friendly. I much prefer someone who wants to hang out after work." What does this have to do with the job?

Q. How do you think your boss will react when you tell her you're leaving?

A. I've already discussed it with her, so she won't be surprised. She doesn't want to lose me, but she knows I'm ready for more responsibility, and she can't offer that to me. The only job with more responsibility than I currently have is hers.

This applicant clearly has a good relationship with his boss.

Never say: "I think she's going to be very upset. I don't know how she's going to replace me." This candidate is being very unrealistic if he thinks he's irreplaceable.

CHAPTER 8

Your Interpersonal Skills

WOULDN'T IT BE NICE IF EVERYONE got along with one another? Unfortunately, a world in which everyone gets along is only a dream. There always will be personality conflicts that lead to differences of opinions, whether they are within families, on the playground, or at work. Differences of opinion cannot be avoided. What is important is how we deal with those different opinions when we encounter them. If handled positively, differences of opinion can lead to new ideas and growth.

An Employee Balancing Act

Each time an employer introduces a new member to his company or department, the delicate balance that existed before is disturbed. Depending on how well the new employee gets along with her new coworkers, this addition may completely tip the scales in one direction or another, or they may move only slightly.

Any change could cause a drop in productivity. An existing employee may find it difficult to concentrate on work when she is worried about what the new coworker meant when she gave her "that look" a few minutes ago. Serious drops in productivity occur when coworkers are too busy arguing to get any work done.

Chapter 3 discussed the personal questions you may be asked on an interview. Employers ask personal questions so they can learn about your personality or character traits. One reason they want to know about this is so they can determine whether you will fit in with the other company employees. These character traits are only a piece of the puzzle, however. A potential employee may have skills and experience that make him the most qualified candidate, but character traits that greatly differ from those of other employees. This probably won't matter to the employer as long as the candidate knows how to make the most of those differences instead of getting sidetracked by them so that productivity suffers.

 FACT

The interviewer will try to find out if you are someone who either causes conflicts or doesn't know how to resolve them. If you indicate that you have a tendency to have problems with conflicts, you won't be hired.

How Do You Resolve Conflicts?

When an employer is trying to find out how you interact with others, she may ask questions about hypothetical situations. For example, you may be asked how you would resolve a problem with a coworker. Alternatively, the interviewer may ask you to discuss times you actually did experience conflict with another individual. You should always present a balanced look at those situations. Everyone knows there are three sides to every story—your side, the other person's side, and the truth. Instead of taking sides, try to offer a look at the situation from everyone's point of view and talk about how you effectively dealt with the problem and solved it. Never place all the blame on anyone else and avoid taking all the blame yourself.

An employer may be interested in knowing how you resolve serious conflicts before they escalate. Too often we hear about an angry employee losing control and doing something to physically harm his employer or coworkers. Your prospective employer will want to know that you are a calm and reasonable person who doesn't let her anger get out of hand. If you are interviewing for a supervisory position, the interviewer will want to know whether you have the ability to defuse the anger of others.

 FACT

According to the U.S. Occupational Safety and Health Administration (OSHA), "Some 2 million American workers are victims of workplace violence each year." ("Workplace Violence," *OSHA Fact Sheet*, 2002. Available from the World Wide Web: *www.osha.gov*)

Q. Unfortunately every office has personality conflicts. What do you do when you work with someone you don't particularly like?

A. While I know you don't have to be buddies with everyone you work with, workplaces are more productive if coworkers get along. I would try to resolve my differences with that person. If that wasn't possible, I'd find something about that person I could admire and respect and I'd focus on that instead of the things I didn't like.

This applicant shows she's proactive when she says she would try to work out her differences with her coworker, but realistic when she says that if she can't, she will find something to respect about her coworker—everyone has redeeming qualities.

Never say: "I get along with everyone, so this won't be a problem." Is this person too good to be true? Probably.

Q. Describe the relationship that should exist between a supervisor and a subordinate.

A. The relationship between a supervisor and a subordinate should be professional, yet friendly. At one of my earlier jobs I had a supervisor who set a perfect example for what this relationship should be like. He always acted professionally but also seemed interested in his workers as people. For example, he made a point of asking us if we had a nice weekend and how things were going, but he never pried into our personal life. He was friendly without trying to be our friend.

This interviewee not only correctly states what the relationship between a supervisor and subordinate should be, but he also talks about his role model for such a relationship.

Never say: "Strictly professional."

Q. What would you do if you disagreed with your boss?

A. It would depend on the situation. If I disagreed with her about whether the office is warm or cold I might not say anything. However, if I disagreed with my boss about whether the new marketing campaign was going to work, I'd share my thoughts with her.

This applicant knows he has to choose his battles wisely. There's a difference between being disagreeable and disagreeing.

Never say: "I would never tell my boss I disagreed with her." This applicant is too passive.

Ⓔ ESSENTIAL

Employers want to hire people who are assertive. They don't want disagreeable employees, but they want those who will speak their minds when necessary.

Q. What do you expect someone you supervise to do if she disagrees with you?

A. I would expect that person to let me know what she's thinking. It could influence my decision. If she doesn't share her thoughts with me, I won't have the opportunity to hear her take on things.

This job candidate respects her coworkers' opinions. She knows it wouldn't be wise to make decisions without taking their comments into consideration.

Never say: "Disagreeing with your supervisor? Isn't that a little disrespectful?" This candidate is more interested in her own image and power than in her company's success.

Q. What would you do if your supervisor handed you an assignment, but you didn't quite understand it?

A. I would first make sure I didn't just need to take a closer look at the project to better understand it. Once I did that, I would ask questions if I needed to. I'd rather ask questions before I begin than have to correct mistakes later on.

This candidate tries to work independently when possible, but knows that clarification is sometimes necessary and is not afraid to ask for it.

Never say: "I would try to figure it out on my own." That may demonstrate independence, but it may also slow things down in the long run.

Q. What would you do if your boss asks you do something that is clearly not part of your job description?

A. It would depend on what it was I was asked to do. I wouldn't expect to run personal errands for my boss, but if I were asked to do something to help the company that wasn't normally part of my job, I wouldn't have a problem with it.

With this answer, the applicant shows his flexibility. However, this extends only to situations where the request is appropriate. If the boss is looking for someone to run his personal errands, and that is something the candidate refuses to do, it's better to set things straight now.

Never say: "I would do anything I was asked to do." While flexibility is important, no one should be a pushover.

Q. How did you get along with your last supervisor?

A. We had a great relationship. I really respected him and I know he respected me, too. He knew he could trust me with any project, so he always assigned me those that were very challenging.

This candidate describes his relationship with his boss on a professional level, and while doing that manages to say something very positive about himself.

Never say: "We got along so well. We had lunch together all the time." It sounds more like this interviewee is describing a buddy than a supervisor.

Q. How do you evaluate the work of others?

A. Giving a critical opinion of someone's work is very tricky. Some people are more receptive than others, so I try to be careful while still getting my point across. I always make sure to talk about what someone has done right before mentioning what he has done wrong. I offer guidance to help my subordinates make the changes they need to, yet give them room to make their own decisions.

This candidate shows that she knows how to handle a potentially sticky situation. She respects her subordinates and wants to maintain a good relationship with them. That, however, doesn't stop her from offering criticism when it is necessary.

Never say: "I'm always straightforward. If someone doesn't want to be criticized, she should do a good job in the first place." A supervisor should know how to be diplomatic. This candidate shows that diplomacy isn't her strong suit.

Q. What would you do if a member of your staff seemed upset about something, but you didn't know what the problem was?

A. I would ask if he wanted to talk about what's bothering him and make sure he knew I was available. If he didn't want to talk, I wouldn't push because it might be something personal. However, if it were work related, I would hope he'd be able to be honest about it so we'd be able to solve the problem together.

This candidate demonstrates both sensitivity and professionalism with this answer. She is sensitive to the needs of her staff and indicates that she is approachable, especially when it comes to work-related issues.

Never say: "I have to maintain a distance between myself and my staff. If there's something I need to know, my employee should come to me. If it's a personal problem, he can just leave it at home where it belongs." This candidate hasn't yet developed an understanding of what it means to be a good manager.

(E) ALERT!

Managers must strike a balance between compassion and professionalism. Employers don't want their management to become so personally involved with staff that it clouds their judgment. On the other hand, they want management to be approachable and understanding.

Q. Have you ever had a boss you didn't like?

A. Of course I've worked for some bosses I've liked more than others, but I try to stay professional and always make an effort to get along with everyone.

"Never complain about a former boss" is the line that keeps running through this candidate's head. Rather than do that, she keeps her answer as positive as possible.

Never say: "Have I ever! Let me tell you about my last boss." This candidate seems eager to talk about her employer behind his back. Is that the kind of person the interviewer wants around his office?

Q. What would you do if your company implemented a policy you disagreed with?

A. Before taking any action I would need to evaluate the situation. I would have to determine whether I just needed time to get used to the new policy or if the policy had serious flaws that would affect the well-being of the company. If I determined that the latter was true, I would express my disapproval as soon as possible. It's difficult to be the one to make waves, but I would have to look out for the company. I wouldn't just criticize the new policy; I would suggest ways to make useful changes.

This interviewee demonstrates that she stops to think before taking action. However, if she determines that she should take action, she does so in a constructive way. She looks out for her employer's welfare and puts the interests of the company first.

Never say: "I don't like making waves. I'd probably just keep my mouth shut." This candidate needs to be more proactive.

Q. What would you do if you received what you felt was an unfair evaluation?

A. I would wait awhile before I approached my supervisor—probably until the next morning. I wouldn't want to talk to my supervisor while I was angry because I might say the wrong thing. I would write down point-by-point why I thought the evaluation was inaccurate. Then I would present my thoughts to my supervisor calmly.

This candidate shows that she does not act on emotion. She takes the time to evaluate a situation before making a move. After doing that she makes an effort to calmly present her case.

Never say: "I'd march right into his office and tell him how wrong he is." The last thing an employer wants is an employee who acts on his emotions. A job candidate should come across as someone who thinks carefully before he acts or speaks.

Q. What would you do if someone you supervised came to you because she felt your evaluation of her was unfair?

A. I would ask her to explain to me why she thought the evaluation was unfair. If she had a valid argument to back up her claim, I would reconsider the evaluation. If not, I would sit down with her to discuss what improvements could be made so that her next evaluation would be better.

This interviewee illustrates how he takes the time to listen to his subordinates. He shows that he is willing to make changes to the evaluation if he realizes he needs to, but if not, will help the employee improve.

Never say: "I'm really careful when I write evaluations, so they are always accurate." This job candidate doesn't realize that everyone can make mistakes, even those who are really careful.

Q. Describe the ideal coworker.

A. The ideal coworker is one who respects those around him. He doesn't engage in behavior that would be offensive to others. He offers constructive criticism and accepts it as well. He contributes to the department and company and doesn't try to compete with his coworkers. He shares responsibility for victories as well as defeats.

This applicant lists a number of desirable qualities and shows that he understands what makes a good employee. Hopefully this candidate is also describing the traits he personally aspires to.

Never say: "I prefer someone who keeps to himself. I really don't want to make friends at work." If this is what this candidate believes, he will have trouble being part of a congenial environment.

Q. Describe the ideal manager.

A. The ideal manager expects a lot of her employees. She respects them. She knows their abilities and makes sure they utilize them to the fullest. She continually challenges them to do more and recognizes their accomplishments.

This answer can mean one of two things. The candidate may be describing her own abilities as a manager. In that case, this is a manager who will retain a productive staff. Alternatively, she could be describing the type of manager she'd like to work under. If that is the case, an employee who likes to work under a supervisor who expects a lot is someone who is willing to live up to those expectations.

Never say: "The ideal manager is one who doesn't interfere too much with her employees. I like someone who just lets everyone do their jobs." If this candidate is describing herself as a manager, she shows that she lacks managerial skills. If she is describing a manager she'd like to work for, she has shown herself as a worker who, for some reason, doesn't want anyone to know what she is doing.

Q. Describe the ideal employee.

A. The ideal employee is one who always does more than she is asked to do. She is open to challenges and is always willing to learn more and take on more responsibilities. She is also receptive to constructive criticism.

Hopefully this candidate has described herself, and any employer would be happy to have an employee like this.

 Never say: "The ideal employee is one who does what is asked of him. He doesn't ask a lot of questions." This candidate, if describing himself, sounds weak.

Ⓔ ESSENTIAL

Every work environment is different, and the interviewer wants to know if you will succeed in his. Employers put a lot of effort into making sure they hire the most suitable candidates possible. The candidate must not only be able to carry out the necessary job duties, but he must fit in well with the other employees.

Q. What would you do if someone came to you to complain about her supervisor?

A. First, I would ask her if she has talked to her supervisor yet. If not, I would ask that she do that first. I would make sure she knew how to approach the supervisor and offer her tips if she didn't. If she has already talked to her supervisor but hasn't gotten anywhere with him, I would have her tell me her side of the story. Next, I would talk to her supervisor to get his side of the story. After considering what both people have told me, I would decide how to resolve the problem.

This job candidate follows protocol by asking the employee to speak to her supervisor first. She demonstrates that she won't take sides and must hear both sides of a story before deciding what to do.

Never say: "I'd listen to what she had to say and then call her supervisor down to my office so I could deal with the problem immediately." This interviewee wastes no time, but this is not the best way to deal with a serious problem.

Q. What would your current coworkers say about you?

A. My coworkers would say I'm very committed to my job. I work hard to contribute to each project's success and I always share credit with everyone else who contributes to that success.

This interviewee portrays himself as someone who is a team player. He sticks to talking about work-related matters.

Never say: "They would say they like me." That's nice, but the applicant should try to think up something a little more concrete to show why he is a good employee.

Q. What would you do about a long-term employee whose work has been slipping lately?

A. I would talk to my employee to find out what was going on. Obviously if this person always did a good job, something must have happened to change that. As a supervisor, it is my job to find out what that is and help the employee fix the problem; it is also preferable to firing someone. It is generally more cost effective to retain a worker who already knows the job than to train someone new. It also is better for the morale of that person's coworkers, who don't want to see a coworker lose his job.

This answer shows that the candidate has good managerial skills. While dismissing an unproductive employee may seem like a quick and easy solution in the short term, it can have a detrimental effect on the company in the end.

Never say: "Whoever doesn't pull his weight has to go. I would just fire the employee." This candidate may know how to solve a problem quickly, but he doesn't account for the repercussions.

Q. What would you do if an important client asked you out on a date?

A. I would politely decline, explaining that I make a point of never mixing business with pleasure. I would then thank her and end the conversation as quickly as possible.

Good answer. This candidate won't compromise his integrity.

Never say: "How important is this client?"

Q. Have you ever had to persuade someone to accept your point of view? How did you do it and were you successful?

A. I have had to do that several times. A few months ago, for example, we were in the process of planning a new publication. We were deciding whether to hire a permanent employee or a freelancer to edit it. My manager felt that we should go with a permanent employee. After analyzing the options, I felt strongly that hiring a freelancer would work best. I presented my reasons for wanting to hire a freelancer, including a cost analysis. I convinced my manager to try it my way, and so far it has worked out very well.

This interviewee gives an example that explains how he gathered information to help him make a decision and then presented the information to his manager to persuade her that this was the best choice.

Never say: "I have. I just talked them into it. I must have the power of persuasion."

Q. How do you handle an angry employee?

A. Way too often you hear about an employee whose anger turns to violence. As a supervisor it would be my job to recognize potentially volatile situations. Once I recognized a problem, I would help the employee remove himself from the situation long enough to cool down. I would tell him where he could go for help, whether through me or a professional counselor.

This applicant knows anger can be serious and what to do before it escalates.

Never say: "I'd fire him." This applicant knows how to escalate a potentially violent situation.

Q. What do you do when you have a very unhappy customer?

A. My first step is to let the customer know I will listen to what he has to say. If the company has a strict policy regarding customer complaints, I will follow it. However, if I must use my own judgment, I will have to strike a balance between keeping the customer happy and not costing my employer too much. If I see that the customer's complaint is legitimate, I will do what it takes to remedy the situation.

This applicant plays by the rules. He knows a satisfied customer will return, but he also realizes that a company is always concerned about its bottom line.

Never say: "The customer is always right. I will just give a customer what they want." If every customer is right, it will cost the company a lot of money.

Ⓔ ESSENTIAL

Employers want to know that those they hire won't drive customers away. They want employees who know how to keep customers satisfied but will be attentive to the company's bottom line and not just hand out free stuff left and right.

Q. A customer is extremely angry because, according to store policy, you can't accept an item he wants to return. How do you handle it?

A. Sometimes you hear about these situations getting out of hand. If it looks like a situation may turn violent, I will do what is necessary to rectify it. If it costs the company a little money, well, the company's bottom line is important, but not as important as people's lives.

This job candidate is practical. She has her priorities in order—lives before money.

✗ **Never say:** "Don't you worry. A customer's anger doesn't scare me. I'll always defend the company's policies." This candidate may be loyal, but her judgment is faulty.

Q. As a supervisor, what do you do when employees working under you don't get along?

A. I actually encountered this situation a few months ago. There were two employees in my department who were both very nice people, but they got off on the wrong foot when one of them transferred into the department. I called a meeting with them and asked them to try to resolve their differences for the good of the department. I can't actually say they like each other now, but there is a level of respect between them.

Nothing is better than a real-life experience. This job candidate was lucky enough to have one he could draw upon. He solved this problem in a very logical way, and was very honest about the outcome.

✗ **Never say:** "It's really none of my business if my employees don't get along." Wrong answer. The interviewer has asked this question for a reason—it is a supervisor's business and he or she must deal with it.

Q. If you were unhappy with your job, how would you discuss this with your boss?

A. I've always had good relationships with everyone I've worked for, so I think it would be to everyone's benefit for me to be direct with my boss. First, I would make a list of the things I'm unhappy with, as well as suggestions for improving each situation. I would then ask for a meeting with my boss to go over the list point by point, being careful not to place any blame.

This interviewee smartly points out that she maintains good relationships with her bosses who can withstand this type of discussion. She explains how she would be proactive in helping to find a solution for the problems she is dealing with at work.

Never say: "I don't think I'd bother discussing it. I would just look for something better." This answer may indicate that this candidate makes rash decisions, and may not be loyal to this job if she gets it.

Q. How do you handle criticism?

A. I think criticism can be a valuable tool. It forces me to take a look at my own work to see how I can improve on it.

This candidate shows that she doesn't get all bent out of shape if someone has an unkind word for her.

Never say: "If someone can't say something nice, maybe they shouldn't say anything at all."

Q. Suppose one of the people you supervise complains that her officemate is slacking off at work. How would you handle it?

A. This happened to me at my last job. I already knew that the supposed slacker actually had higher productivity than the employee who complained, so I know it's important to take such a complaint with a grain of salt. If this happened again I would politely tell the employee that I would handle the situation if necessary. Then I would keep an eye on the complainer, who apparently has too much time on her hands.

This manager portrays herself as someone who is very observant and is aware of what her staff is doing. She also handles the situation well by politely putting her employee in her place.

Never say: "I would tell her to mind her own business." An effective supervisor needs to have a little more tact than that.

Q. What would you do with an employee who seems to do his work very slowly? She gets her work done on time, but it's always very close to the deadline.

A. Some people work more slowly than others. If her work is accurate and it's being completed before the deadline, I don't think there's anything to worry about.

The interviewee is very practical. She knows that everyone has different work styles and working quickly doesn't necessarily mean better performance.

Never say: "I'd ask her to speed up and start asking for progress reports." This candidate sounds like someone who will cause unnecessary tension among the people she supervises.

Q. The person in the next cubicle spends endless hours on the phone talking to his girlfriend. Not only is he not getting his work done, but his chatter is keeping you from doing yours. What do you do?

A. I would talk to him before I did anything else. He may not realize how loud his phone conversations are. I would politely let him know that I can hear what he's saying and hopefully that would be enough to get him to lower his volume. I might also consider getting a noise machine—something that plays soothing sounds—to block out his voice. If nothing else helped, I would try to move to another cubicle.

This job candidate shows that he's determined to solve problems on his own before involving his supervisor.

Never say: "I would tell my supervisor. Who does this guy think he is, talking on the phone instead of working?" The prospective employer will see this interviewer as someone who will make waves. He has better things to do than worry about helping his employees solve petty disputes.

Ⓔ ALERT!

Show that you can resolve problems on your own. A candidate who indicates that he will go running to his supervisor to report difficulties with a coworker will be viewed by the interviewer as too "high maintenance."

CHAPTER 9

Did You Do Your Homework?

IN CHAPTER 1 YOU WERE TOLD that researching a prospective employer is one of the most important things you can do to prepare for a job interview. You were told to find out about the company's line of business, its financial condition, its customers and clients, and the industry in which the company operates, including the latest news. Here's where that research will come in handy. Arriving at the interview prepared with this information shows the prospective employer how serious you are about the interview and about the job.

Proving Your Knowledge

An interviewer will ask you to discuss what you know about her company and about the particular job you are interviewing for. Obviously the interviewer is not asking you for this information because she wants or needs it herself. She wants to know that you spent time doing the research to get this information.

Why does the interviewer want to make sure you've done this research? A job candidate who walks into an interview armed with knowledge about the employer demonstrates several things to the interviewer. He demonstrates that he isn't just looking for a job with *any* employer. He wants to work for this particular company because of what he knows about it. He also shows that he was ambitious enough to do the necessary research to learn what he could about the employer.

The interviewer may ask you direct questions regarding what you know about the company. If you haven't done your research, you won't be able to answer these questions. He will ask you about the company's services and its products. He may also ask you to talk about the industry the company is part of.

 ESSENTIAL

To find basic information about a prospective employer, start by looking at the company's Web site. You can learn about a company's product line and key personnel. Public companies often make their annual reports available on their Web sites. Some also provide a list of clients.

The interviewer may also ask you questions that aren't as straightforward. You may not even realize at first that he is testing your knowledge about the company. For example, the interviewer may ask you what you can contribute to the company and what changes you would make if you were hired. He may ask you why you want to work for the company and how it fits into your career plans. Using your research, base your answers to these questions upon what you know about the company.

Highlight Skills That Fit the Company

Throughout a job interview you will be asked many questions about your skills, work history, and accomplishments. The interviewer will ask you these questions because she wants to know what you can bring to her company. While it is possible to answer these questions without using any information about the company, displaying your knowledge by drawing on specific facts will set you apart from the other candidates who are competing for the job.

Knowing factual information about the company and the position allows you to tailor your answers so you can show why you will be a valuable employee. For example, when the interviewer asks you questions about your skills, you not only will be able to talk about the ones you have, you also will be able to talk about how they will benefit the company based on what you know about it. When you are asked about your work history, again you will be able to talk about experience related to the job you are being interviewed for. When you discuss your accomplishments, you will present them in a way that lets the employer see how you will potentially have similar accomplishments at his company.

 FACT

The United States Bureau of Labor Statistics (BLS) publishes industry information online. For example, Industry at a Glance (✐*www.bls.gov/iag/iaghome.htm*) is a helpful resource with links to profiles of twelve industry supersectors, including education and health services, professional and business services, and wholesale and retail trade.

Q. Now that you've told me about yourself, can you tell me what you know about us?

A. Costello Laboratories is a pharmaceutical company with annual sales of over $15 billion. The company recently introduced a new medication to treat bipolar disorder, and I read that it is working on a new cardiac medication.

This answer shows that this candidate has done her homework. She knows what the company does and has even kept up with the latest news.

Never say: "I haven't been able to find out anything about it." Other than being called for an interview an hour before it is to take place, there is no excuse for not doing your homework.

Q. What do you think it takes to be successful here?

A. I understand that Q & H Corporation introduced five new products to the market in the last year alone. In order to be a successful employee of such an innovative company, one would have to be very creative. In a competitive industry such as soaps and toiletries you need employees who can keep up with what consumers want.

This person has obviously done her homework. She not only knows about the company, but she seems to know about the industry as well.

Never say: "In order to be successful, employees must work hard and do a good job." This can be said of employees of any company. If this candidate had done her homework, she would know more about this particular company.

Q. Based on what you know about this company, how will you contribute to it?

A. I see that most of your company's clients are in the food industry. Since I spent ten years working for AMJ Bean Company, I am very familiar with that industry. I know my experience in the industry is something your clients will appreciate.

This candidate has researched her prospective employer and knows that her experience in the food industry will help her should she be hired. She is able to make a point of mentioning that on the job interview.

Never say: "I have great organizational skills and I can manage my time well." While most employers value these skills, the candidate does not explain why they will benefit this particular company.

Q. There are a lot of companies that can use someone with your skills. Why do you want to work at this company?

A. Home Warehouse has been more successful than any other company in the hardware industry. The company has seen steady profit growth over many years and it appears it will continue to do so. However, critics of the company are quick to point out that customer service is seriously lacking. As the director of customer service I will implement new procedures that will turn that negative image around.

This answer shows the interviewee's knowledge of the company, including its weaknesses. He already has a plan in mind to fix that weakness, as he shares with the interviewer.

Never say: "I heard you pay really well." This candidate shows that he doesn't really know a lot about the company and how he will fit in as an employee.

Q. What do you know about this industry?

A. The retail industry is tremendous. As a matter of fact, it is the second largest industry in the United States, both in terms of number of establishments and of employees. There has been a decline in sales over recent years, but industry analysts think that will turn around when the economy improves.

This job candidate has done enough research to be able to intelligently discuss what he knows about the industry.

Never say: "I don't know a lot about the retail industry. I've only worked in the financial industry, so this is all new to me." Knowledge about an industry does not have to come from experience. There are many resources this interviewee could have accessed to gather information.

Q. Why do you want to work in this industry?

A. I'm ready for a new challenge, and since more commercial banks have begun to offer investment services over the last few years, I know I can use the skills I learned as an investment banker to work in the commercial banking industry.

By giving this answer, the interviewee is able to demonstrate that she knows about this industry and what she can bring to it.

Never say: "The hours are much better than they are in the investment banking industry." This answer doesn't show that the interviewee knows more about the industry than the number of hours one must work, and it certainly doesn't show what she can bring to it.

Q. How much do you know about our company's recent growth?

A. I know that XYZ Brands is a multinational company. I was particularly intrigued by your acquisition of ABC Corporation last March. It seems like it's going to open up a whole new market for this company.

Not only does the interviewee show that she took the time to learn about the company, she also shows she's kept up with the latest news about it. Notice that the interviewee said "it's going to open up a whole new market for this company" not "your company," so as not to create distance between herself and the employer.

Never say: "I see your commercials on TV all the time, so you must be a pretty big company."

Q. What interests you about our products and services?

A. Turning Corporation provides products and services that help so many people. Just the other day I was reading about the new motorized scooter Turning developed. Those in health care and advocates for the disabled are very excited about it, according to everything I've read.

This candidate has obviously made a point of learning about her prospective employer, including keeping up with news about the latest products.

Never say: "I don't know much about your products, but by the looks of your offices, they must sell really well."

Q. Is there anything you've heard about our company that you don't like?

A. It's really nothing specific to your company. I know the industry is a little shaky now, so of course I have some concerns about that. Based on what I've been reading, though, it looks like things are improving some.

This candidate shows that she did her homework, yet avoids bringing up anything that may cause awkward feelings. However, if there was something splashed across the front page of newspapers, the candidate would look ignorant if she didn't talk about it.

Never say: "I heard that you fire people who don't agree with you. Is that true?" That is something that might only be rumor. Bringing it up during the interview could cause a lot of embarrassment.

Q. Is there anything you find troubling about this industry?

A. Actually, no. I've been reading a lot about this industry and everything I've seen so far is positive. This industry has made a great recovery after the decline about a decade ago. Since then it has been growing steadily and actually saw record growth last year.

Although she doesn't have anything negative to say, this candidate takes this opportunity to show that she did her homework.

Never say: "No. It's nice to be in an industry like this, isn't it?" This interviewee may have done her homework, but she needs to elaborate to prove that.

Q. Where do you think this company is going to be in five years?

A. Based on what I've been reading it seems this company will be fully expanded into the international market by then. Parker Corporation opened offices in Japan and Switzerland last year, and I read that they are looking into opening Canadian offices next year.

This candidate is aware of what his prospective employer has in store for the future because he did his homework.

Never say: "The future is always so fuzzy. Who can ever predict what is going to happen?" This interviewer didn't ask this candidate to look into a crystal ball. She wants him to make a prediction based on his current knowledge.

Q. Do you know what your job duties will be if we hire you?

A. As eligibility clerk, I know I will use my interviewing skills to help determine whether individuals are eligible to receive assistance from various government programs. I will interview people and then write reports that will be sent to the appropriate agencies.

This candidate knows what the general duties are for the job.

Never say: "I didn't get a chance to look into that." The interviewer will wonder how this candidate can interview for a job he knows nothing about.

Q. How does this job fit in with your career goals?

A. As I mentioned earlier, my long-range goal is to be an elementary school principal. Reaching that is several years off, of course. I have a lot to learn about school administration. I've attended several workshops you've run and I am always impressed by your knowledge, and I know I can learn a lot from you. From what I've heard through the grapevine, you always place a lot of trust in everyone you hire and give employees a chance to grow. I know I can gain valuable knowledge and experience here at Oakwood, in addition to what I can contribute as an assistant principal.

This candidate demonstrates her knowledge about her prospective employer. She has personally learned from him in the past. She has also talked to other people who know him and how the school is run.

Never say: "It's an assistant principal job and clearly it's the next step I need to take in order to become a principal." In other words, this interviewee doesn't care where she gets her experience as long as she gets it.

Q. What do you know about some of our major clients?

A. I know your major clients are all in the canned food industry. BBR represents Heller Foods, Green Products, and Acorn Corp. I read in *Advertising Digest* just last week that Heans hired you to run their new broadcast campaign.

This candidate has done his homework, even keeping up with the latest industry news.

Never say: "I haven't had a chance to find out who they are."

Q. If we hire you, what aspect of this job do you think you'll like best? What aspect of the job will you like least?

A. I will enjoy working with clients one-on-one best, as I have in my previous position. The part I will like least is completing the massive quantity of paperwork that is required by all government agencies. However, I know it's a necessary part of this job and I've learned that if you keep up with it, it is much easier to deal with.

Demonstrating what he knows about the job, this candidate is able to discuss what he likes and doesn't like about it. He picks the major part of his job, working with clients, as the thing he likes best. When saying what he doesn't enjoy, he is upbeat and quick to point out that he knows it is necessary.

Never say: "I love working with clients but I hate doing all the paperwork." It would have been better for this candidate not to be so vehement about his dislike of paperwork.

Q. What would you like to accomplish here if we hire you?

A. I read that this company is expanding into the children's clothing market. With my background in that area, I know I can help make that clothing line successful.

The interviewee bases his answer on what he has learned about this employer. He explains how his experience will help the company reach its goals.

Never say: "I hope to move up to the executive suite." The candidate may have researched the layout of the office to determine that this suite exists, but that's not exactly the type of research that will impress a prospective employer.

Q. Since all your experience has been in another industry, you must be a little concerned about making this change. What do you think working in this industry will be like?

A. Everything in this industry seems to go at a very fast pace. I think the transition will be an easy one for me because in the magazine industry, I also worked at a fast pace. There were tight deadlines and sudden changes that needed to be dealt with on a moment's notice. From what I can tell, this industry involves the same things. I think I will be able to make a seamless transition to this industry.

This candidate's answer conveys that he feels he can adapt to working in this new industry.

Never say: "I think it will be fine." This candidate needs to explain why he feels that way.

Q. What do you think will be different about working for this company than working for your current employer?

A. My current employer sells home furnishings, while this company sells office furnishings. This means I will work with a different group of clients and new products; however, I can utilize my skills as a decorator and as a salesperson here as I do with my current employer.

This candidate knows enough about her prospective employer to answer this question. She makes a point of discussing how her skills can be used to work with a different product and different clientele.

Never say: "It's a much shorter commute." This may be true, but it doesn't really have much to do with what this candidate can bring to this employer.

Q. Describe your ideal job.

A. Ideally, I'd like to work as a senior project manager overseeing the development of housing complexes.

This candidate is interviewing for a job that will eventually lead to the one that she is describing.

Never say: "I'd love to teach one day." It's nice to have career aspirations, but they should at least be related to the job you are applying for.

Ⓔ ESSENTIAL

When you are asked to describe your ideal job, you should talk about one that is on your career path. You don't want to describe a job that is unrelated to the one you are applying for.

Q. Describe your ideal company to work for.

A. I'd like to work for a software company where I will have the opportunity to contribute to the business by utilizing my programming skills as well as my teaching abilities.

This interviewee describes the potential employer's company. He makes sure to point out what he can bring to the job.

Never say: "I'd really like to work for a big company but none of them are hiring right now." Honesty isn't always the best policy.

Q. Our latest venture has been all over the news. What would you do to make the transition go more smoothly for our employees?

A. I would make sure employees know how the merger between this company and Pacific Pencil Company will affect them. I would hold meetings to discuss how procedures will change and schedule workshops to help employees adapt to these changes. When my former employer merged with RQR International, I assisted the vice president who was responsible for handling the transition, so I have experience in this area.

By referring to the venture by name, this candidate shows he knows what the interviewer is talking about. He has clearly given some thought to how this merger will affect the company and knows how to deal with it, and he can draw upon his experience with a similar situation.

Never say: "What venture is that? I haven't had time lately to pay attention to the news."

Q. Can you define this position as you understand it?

A. This position involves supervising a staff of about fifty-five data entry clerks. I would be responsible for scheduling employees, delegating work assignments, and quality control.

This candidate understands the job she is interviewing for. She has read the job announcement and has listened carefully during the interview.

Never say: "Data entry supervisor." Good. The candidate knows the title of the job she is interviewing for. However, she needs to elaborate to show she knows what she's getting into.

Q. Are you available during the hours we're open?

A. Yes, I am. I took a look at your Web site and saw that the library provides service Monday through Saturday, from 9 A.M. to 9 P.M. I'm available during all those times.

This interviewee knows what the hours are and can commit to working when she is needed.

 Never say: "What hours are you open?"

Ⓔ ALERT!

An employer should not ask if you are unable to work on a particular day due to religious observance. The Civil Rights Act of 1964 prohibits employment discrimination on the basis of religion.

Q. You are aware you will have to relocate if we hire you. Do you think you will like living here?

A. I've done some research about this city and I think it would be a great place to live. The crime rate is pretty low and the climate is just about perfect. There are so many museums and theaters here, it won't be hard to find something to do on my time off.

This answer proves that this candidate has done his research and learned as much as he could about this city.

Never say: "I can be happy anywhere." This interviewee may show that he is flexible, but since he didn't do any research into moving to a new location, this prospective employer may not see him as someone who is committed to making a permanent move.

Q. I see from your resume that you were a member of Students Against Teen Smoking. Since one of the largest tobacco companies is our major client, will your anti-smoking stance pose a problem for you when dealing with this company?

A. When I first discovered that Burnz Corporation was one of Krull Media's clients, I hesitated to apply. I decided to do some research to learn more about Burnz and found out that the company has never marketed its product to teens or tried to make it appealing to them in any way. Actually, I saw the campaign the company ran last year that addressed the issue of underage smoking. I understand your agency worked on that campaign.

This candidate did research in order to learn about his prospective employer. In doing so, he learned that he might have philosophical differences with one of the employer's clients. Not wanting to compromise his principles or take himself out of the running for the job, he did more research to help him learn more about the client in question.

Never say: "I had no idea one of this company's clients was a tobacco company." Had this candidate known that, he would have been able to make an educated decision about whether to even interview for the job.

Q. Do you know who our major competitors are?

A. Yes, I do. There are four big names in the communications industry. There's BCD, DRG, Parrot, and of course, this company, Chime.

This candidate has done his homework.

Never say: "Nope."

Q. Would you rather be a big fish in a small pond or a small fish in a big pond?

A. I would much rather be a big fish in a small pond. Working for a small company provides me with the opportunity to use more of my skills. I like it when my job duties are diversified. Most of my experience has been with small companies, so I understand the unique challenges that can come up. For example, I know how to be careful when scheduling out-of-town business meetings so there are always enough people in the office to deal with emergencies that come up.

This candidate is interviewing for a job in a small company. She explains why this is a better fit for her.

Never say: "Whichever." This candidate should use this opportunity to explain why she is a good fit for this employer.

Q. How well do you understand our mission?

A. From my research, I understand that your mission is to develop high-quality toys that enhance learning and provide entertainment for children between preschool age and ten years old.

This candidate states the company's mission as she understands it, which is exactly what the interviewer asked her to do.

Never say: "I haven't had a chance to do much research about it, but I know you sell toys." While you may not always be able to find out what a company's mission is, you should at least try to do the research.

Q. If you were interviewing potential employees for a job here, how would you describe this organization to them?

A. XRT, Inc., manufacturers windows and sells them directly to the consumer. The company has a sales force of about twenty people who respond to customer inquiries by visiting their homes or places of business.

This answer shows that this interviewee has a firm grasp of what this business is all about.

Never say: "It's a window company in Chicago." This answer doesn't prove that this candidate knows much about this company.

Q. If you had the opportunity to develop a new product to add to our line, what would it be?

A. Since Perfect Posies currently sells flowers and other gift items, I think a line of chocolate would be a good choice. I recently saw a survey that said that consumers spend $150 billion on chocolate gifts each year, so this would be a great market to enter. And since this company already has a great reputation in the mail-order gift industry and the systems in place to handle the addition of this product, this would be a natural expansion of Perfect Posies' product line.

This is a well-thought-out answer based on this candidate's knowledge of the company and the gift industry in general.

Never say: "I don't know much about your current line. Do you offer anything besides flowers yet?"

CHAPTER 10

What Would You Do If You Were Hired?

WHEN A PROSPECTIVE EMPLOYER LOOKS AT YOU, she sees you in three ways—past, present, and future. Your work history and your education make up your past. Your personality, strengths and weaknesses, and skills make up your present, or who you are today. Finally, a prospective employer wants to know the future—that is, what you would do if she hires you. Without a crystal ball, she must ask a lot of questions in order to get a clearer picture.

What You Can Bring to a Company

The interviewer's primary concern is to find out if you will be able to carry out the duties of the job. In most situations, you will have had the opportunity to read a job description in advance of your interview. If not, do your best to determine what the typical job duties are for the position you are applying for. You should be ready to explain why you are qualified to carry out each duty.

A prospective employer might talk about some specific projects he has in store for his new hire. He will want you to discuss how you will approach those projects. This would be a good time to discuss how you approached similar projects in the past. You will most likely also be asked a number of questions about hypothetical situations. Whenever possible, draw on your past experiences to illustrate your skills for dealing with each situation.

ESSENTIAL

Arm yourself with a cache of examples that make you the most qualified candidate for the job. These examples will come from your work experience, and in lieu of that, from your experience as a student, whether in class or through your participation in extracurricular activities.

What the Company Expects of You

Every employer expects different things of his or her employees. Some need you to work long hours on a regular basis, while other jobs require employees to work late occasionally, perhaps during a particular busy season. Some jobs involve frequent travel. There are other jobs that require you to be on call during weekends. If any of these are a part of the position you are interviewing for, you will be asked whether or not you will have a problem meeting such requirements.

It is in your best interests to be honest about what you are willing to do regarding traveling and working late. If you know you must pay your dues and will be amenable to doing whatever is asked of you, then by all means indicate that during the interview. However, if you are not, you should let the employer know right away.

 ALERT!

When you are asked about your willingness to travel or work late, saying you can't do it will take you out of the running for the job. With that in mind, speak up only if you are absolutely positive that you will not be willing to do something.

A job interview is a tool you can use to determine whether a job is right for you. If you are not willing to work late or travel, or do something else the interviewer suggests will be required, then you have just discovered the job is not right for you, and you should speak up. If there are extenuating circumstances, for example, if you can't work late because of another obligation but you can come in early and are willing to do so, bring that up. Your prospective employer may be able to work within the parameters of your schedule.

As the prospective employer is asking you about what you will do if you are hired, she may also want to find out what your salary requirements are. During the interview you are better off talking about the typical salary range in your field, leaving an extensive discussion of specifics for when the employer makes a job offer.

Q. The department you would be in charge of hasn't had a supervisor in months. This is going to be a big transition for the staff. How will you handle it?

A. I wouldn't want to make any big changes for at least the first two weeks. I find it's better to just observe how things are done before trying to make any improvements. I want to gain the staff's trust first and listen to their concerns.

This candidate has a plan in place and she lays it out step by step. She knows that employees who have been unsupervised for a long time need to get used to having someone overseeing their work.

Never say: "Well, the first thing I would do is make some changes around here. If there hasn't been a supervisor running things for a while, things are sure to be messed up."

Q. The person who fills this position will have to work on his own most of the time. Can you handle that?

A. I am used to working independently. On my last job, I edited the company newsletter. I was responsible for compiling the material, writing the articles, and preparing the newsletter for publication each quarter. I had to set my own deadlines for each step along the way.

This candidate explains how a project he was responsible for prepared him to work independently.

Never say: "I love working on my own. It's less distracting." This answer shows that this candidate may be able to work on his own, but he's inflexible. If he had to work with others, could he?

Q. How do you feel about working long hours?

A. Can you explain what you mean by long hours? Does that mean working late or getting to work early?

The applicant knows she already has a commitment two nights a week. She doesn't mind getting to work early, though. She decides it's better to find out what her prospective employer's expectations are before she rules anything out or commits to something she won't be able to follow through with.

Never say: "I love working long hours. It means I don't have to go home and deal with my family." Even if the applicant is trying to be funny, this is not the place to bring up personal issues.

 ESSENTIAL

> If you don't understand a question or just need something clarified, it's okay to ask questions during the interview. It is preferable to saying more than needs to be said, or giving a response that doesn't answer the question.

Q. Our culture here is casual. I see you've worn a suit today. How would you dress for work if I hire you?

A. I would adhere to the culture of this company and would dress in slacks and a nice shirt.

This candidate knows it's important to fit in with the culture of the workplace. He also knows that casual doesn't mean jeans and a T-shirt.

Never say: "I feel more comfortable in a suit."

Q. Senior citizens represent a huge market now and we want to convince them to buy our product. If we hired you, how would you help with that?

A. In addition to being a very big market, the senior market also continues to grow. They are a group with a very active lifestyle. Many have expendable income and they choose to use their savings on travel, so it's clear we have a product they will want. We have to determine how to reach them. I would first want to do research to find out what publications seniors read and what television shows they watch. Only then can we embark on an advertising campaign.

This candidate demonstrates that he would take a methodical approach to this project. He also shows that he understands the market very well.

Never say: "Seniors don't have a lot of money to spend, so why would we target them?" This interviewee doesn't know the market and contradicts the interviewer.

Q. We're about to change over to a new software program for our shipping and receiving department. We'd like the person we hire for this position to do the training. Are you the right person for that job?

A. I am definitely the right person for this job. As you can see on my resume, my last job was with a software distributor. One of my responsibilities was to travel to our clients' offices to provide software training.

This is one confident candidate.

Never say: "Um, I did some training." This applicant doesn't sound very confident.

Q. In about a year we want to open a new branch on the other side of town. We plan to train the person who takes this position to run that office. Is that something you'd be interested in?

A. I would welcome that opportunity if it arises.

Notice the applicant says, "If it arises." She wants to express her eagerness to take on more responsibility with this employer without sounding like she'd leave if that opportunity didn't come up, or if such an opportunity came up sooner with another company.

Never say: "That's exactly what I'm looking for." This candidate sounds like she would leave if the company's plans changed. Also, the manager may question this candidate's interest in the position she is currently interviewing for.

Q. If we hire you, will you be willing to get your certification? You have all the skills we're looking for, but we really need someone who is certified.

A. I was planning to take my certification exam in June. That's the next time it's being given.

While it would have been okay for this candidate to say he would get his certification because the client has asked him to, it's even better that he said he was planning to do it anyway.

Never say: "I don't understand why certification matters so much, but if you need me to do it I will." Show some enthusiasm, please.

Q. The person who last held this position took ill and has only been able to work off and on for the last three months and has finally resigned. Things are a huge mess, which the person we hire will need to sort out. Are you up for the challenge?

A. I love a good challenge. First I'll sort through the mess to organize it. Then I'll see which things require immediate attention and which things I can work on later.

The interviewee, by giving this answer, shows that she knows how to both organize and prioritize. These are two skills that are extremely important for someone taking over a job that has been neglected.

Never say: "I'm sure once I see the mess I can figure out what to do with it." Even though this candidate shows confidence, she doesn't have a plan.

Q. The person we hire will have to respond to customer complaints occasionally. Will you be able to do that?

A. Years ago I worked in customer service. I'll be able to put that experience to good use.

The interviewee finds some past experience that will help her with this aspect of the job.

Never say: "I'm sure it won't be too big a deal." If the interviewer bothered to ask this question, it may be a big deal.

Q. We often work on teams here. Would you rather work on a team or on your own?

A. I work well independently and on a team. On my previous jobs I've had to do both. We often worked on teams to complete larger projects. I like how working on a team allows you to draw on the strength of each of its members.

This interviewee shows that he is flexible enough to work on either a team or independently, but addresses the focus of the question by emphasizing his teamwork skills.

Never say: "On a team, of course." This candidate just says what he thinks the interviewer wants to hear, without giving any proof to back up his answer.

Q. We have several clients with outstanding bills. If we hire you, how will you handle this situation?

A. First, I would want to go through the paperwork to make sure these clients were properly notified their accounts are delinquent. If I find out they were notified, I'll call each one personally to discuss this. There might be extenuating circumstances. It's important not to be too heavy-handed in dealing with these types of situations. After all, these are our clients. We don't want to lose them entirely.

This candidate gives a clearly thought-out answer. She knows how important it is to be diplomatic when dealing with clients.

Never say: "My first priority would be getting on the phone and getting payment from them as quickly as possible." While this might work, it would also alienate clients.

Q. Our clients expect a very quick turnaround on the projects we do for them. Can you handle that?

A. Yes, I can. While I was in graduate school, I had several professors who assigned projects that were due only a few days later. I became an expert at scheduling my time around completing these assignments.

Since this interviewee doesn't have work experience to draw upon, she talks about her experience as a student. In the process she highlights a valuable skill—time management.

Never say: "I'm sure I can." This interviewee needs to give a specific example or, in the absence of one, talk about any skills she possesses that will help her.

Q. If you are hired for this position, you will go from managing your current staff of ten to managing fifty people. Will you be able to oversee a substantially larger staff?

A. Yes, I will. Although I've never managed a staff of that size before, I know I have the skills necessary to do it. I am a strong leader. I am good at communicating what each member of my staff needs to accomplish. I am good at delegating responsibilities, which will be even more important with such a large staff.

This candidate lets the interviewer know that he has all the skills that a good manager should have, even though he doesn't have experience with the exact situation he will face.

Never say: "Since I've never managed such a big staff, I might find it overwhelming. I'm sure I'll be able to handle it, though." This interviewee focuses on the negative rather than on why he can handle the job despite his lack of experience. He should never mention feeling overwhelmed.

Q. We're implementing a new computer system in this department. If we hire you for this position, you'll need to spend a month in Seattle learning how to use it. Are you okay with that?

A. That would be fine.

***

This was a yes or no question. The interviewee doesn't need to say any more than this.

Never say: "That sounds great, but do you know when that would be? It rains a lot in Seattle and I hate the rain. Don't you?" This candidate has said way too much.

Q. When we are in the process of developing a new product, it's essential that information about it doesn't leak out. How are you at keeping secrets?

A. After working in the technology field for the last three years, I know how important it is to keep information confidential until a product is released.

***

This candidate knows from experience that keeping secrets is important.

Never say: "Wouldn't I have to sign a confidentiality agreement or something?" Is threat of being sued for breach of contract the only thing that would keep this applicant quiet?

 FACT

Companies are always racing to release new products before the competition. They expect their employees to keep any information they learn about the new product behind company doors.

Q. We currently have several employees who have problems with things like tardiness and excessive personal phone calls. How would you deal with this if we hired you as supervisor?

A. First, I would need to find out exactly what is occurring. Then, prior to singling out any one employee, I would circulate a memo to the entire department that reiterated the rules. If the behavior continued, I would have a private meeting with each employee who isn't following the rules. I would stress the importance of following the rule they are breaking, and try to find out if there are extenuating circumstances that could be remedied. If the employee continues to break the rules, there would be repercussions.

This interviewee is clearly not one to "leap without looking." She knows how important it is to evaluate a situation before taking action. However, she will take action in an expedient manner.

Never say: "You won't have to worry about anyone breaking the rules once I take over." This candidate must put forth a series of steps she will take to remedy the situation.

Q. Four times a year we work around the clock for about a week. Will that be a problem?

A. That's fine with me. I understand that the beginning of each season is a very busy time.

Not only is this job candidate willing to work late, he knows enough about the industry to know what times of year this would be expected of him.

Never say: "Do you let people take vacation during those times?" He hasn't even started and he sounds like he's trying to wiggle out of responsibility.

Q. As my assistant, would I be able to trust you to take over for me whenever I'm out of the office?

A. Absolutely. I would follow whatever rules you set forth. I also have excellent judgment, so I can handle whatever comes up.

The applicant uses this opportunity to highlight her skills.

Never say: "Does that happen a lot?" Just answer the question.

Q. Whoever fills this position will need to write next year's budget, which needs to be 10 percent lower than the current one. Could you do this?

A. I had to do something similar when my department went through funding cuts last year and I was in charge of writing the new budget. First I reviewed the current year's budget and removed amounts that had been budgeted for one-time events. Then I found a few areas where our actual expenditures were lower than we had budgeted for, and I was able to bring the amount down to more realistic levels, of course accounting for possible price increases. Finally, I went through it to see what cuts would have a minimal effect on services. I cut a program that traditionally had very low attendance. This eliminated the need to hire a part-time instructor. I was able to submit a budget that was 12 percent lower than the one for the previous year.

This candidate demonstrates how he takes a practical approach to trimming a budget. He shows how he is able to get the job done with a minimal effect on service.

Never say: "Some of the budget cuts I make may be unpopular, but saving the agency money is my priority." It's true that saving money is important. However, there are consequences of making radical cuts that will affect service.

Q. This job requires some travel. Is that a problem?

A. I understand that traveling is common in this industry and that's fine with me. I look forward to representing this company around the country.

***

This candidate has done her homework and wisely speaks of herself as if she has the job.

Never say: "I love traveling. There are so many places I want to visit." This candidate's mistake is talking about how she will benefit from traveling rather than talking about how her traveling will benefit her prospective employer.

Q. The students in this school can be very challenging to manage. As a teacher here, will you be able to handle them?

A. I worked with special-needs children when I was an assistant teacher at Ardsley School. I learned that it is important to look at each child as an individual. Each one has different strengths and weaknesses. If you look at it that way, you can figure out what strategy you need to use to work with each child. Children will trust you when they know you see them as individuals and will usually respond by doing what you need them to do.

***

Although this candidate is applying for his first professional job, he is able to draw on his past experience. He explains what he learned from his previous experience as an assistant teacher.

Never say: "I'm a strict disciplinarian, so this won't be a problem." This answer doesn't demonstrate that this interviewee has a strategy for dealing with difficult children.

Q. Anyone who takes this position will need to handle stress well. Are you good at handling stress?

A. Yes, I am. My last job was very stressful, but I found that practicing some relaxation techniques like deep breathing helped me combat the stress. I also made sure to take a lunch break every day, since that gives me time to regroup and start the rest of my day with a positive attitude.

This candidate demonstrates that she has strategies in place to help her deal with stress.

Never say: "If you love your job, you don't find it stressful." That is unrealistic. Even if you love your job, it can be stressful at times. Those who have a coping mechanism will be better able to deal with stressful situations.

Q. In this fast-paced environment we need someone who can think on her feet. Are you that person?

A. Yes, I am. I have experience making thoughtful decisions under pressure. I worked at a daily newspaper for five years. Every day we had to make last-minute decisions about what to include in the next day's edition. There was no time to waste when the paper had to go to press within the next half-hour.

This candidate shows how her experience has enabled her to be decisive.

Never say: "Uhm . . . well, let me think about this. . . . Let's see . . . hmm . . ." This candidate doesn't need to say anything else. The interviewer has his answer.

Q. Each employee in this department is on call one weekend a month. How do you feel about that?

A. That is fine with me.

All that's needed is a simple yes or no.

Never say: "Would I get paid for being on call?" That question can wait until a job offer is made and salary is negotiated.

(E) ALERT!

> If your religious beliefs prevent you from working on Saturday or Sunday, you can say you have a prior obligation for one day over the weekend but would be happy to work the other day. Remember that an employer must reasonably accommodate employees' sincerely held religious beliefs and cannot base his or her decision to hire you on your religion. If you wanted to reveal that information, it couldn't be held against you.

Q. Are you willing to work late occasionally?

A. I know what it's like when a deadline is coming up. In my last job I was asked to work late from time to time. It was never a problem for me. When a deadline is quickly approaching, I'll be able to make sure we meet it.

By giving this answer, the interviewee not only uses language that puts himself in the position that he's interviewing for, but also tells his prospective boss that he's worked late in the past.

Never say: "I'll work late every night if you want me to." Is this interviewee just saying what he thinks the interviewer wants to hear?

Q. As a contact person for our clients, you might have to tell them little white lies to keep them happy. For example, we never would want a client to know about a mishap that occurred with a project we were working on for them. Would you be comfortable with that?

A. I'm always inclined to be honest. However, I know that little white lies come with the territory in this field. If not telling a client the whole truth keeps them calm and happy, then I can do that. No need to worry anyone unnecessarily. Of course, I will work to make sure the problem is resolved as quickly as possible.

Knowing what common practice is in her field helps this candidate answer this question. By telling the interviewer that she always tries to be honest but is willing to tell a client a white lie to keep him happy, she essentially says to the interviewer, "I'll always be honest with you, but I'll also help protect your relationship with clients even if it means telling the occasional half-truth."

Never say: "I never ever tell lies. It's wrong." This candidate may not know the field well enough to give the correct answer. While it may sound virtuous to never tell lies, she doesn't realize that not being totally truthful may sometimes be necessary.

Q. It's getting too expensive to operate a business in this city. Would you be willing to relocate?

A. I'd be willing to relocate anywhere within the United States.

This candidate gives an honest answer.

Never say: "I love to move around, so that's really good news." This applicant doesn't sound like stability is his strong suit.

Q. What salary are you looking for?

A. From my research, I know the salary range for those with my experience working in this industry here in New York is $51,000 to $55,000. I'm confident we can agree on a salary that is acceptable.

⟨ ⟩

This applicant has done her homework. She gives a range rather than an absolute number, showing her flexibility.

Never say: "I have to make $52,000."

Ⓔ ALERT!

Job candidates should not bring up any questions about salary until after the employer makes a job offer. If the interviewer brings it up, the candidate should avoid giving an absolute number, but should instead give a range.

Q. I see from the salary history you sent that you were earning $45,000 on your last job. We've taken some losses over the last year and won't be able to pay you that. Will that be a problem?

A. I'm sure we can agree on a reasonable salary.

⟨ ⟩

This applicant knows it's better to discuss salary after the employer makes an offer.

Never say: "How much less than that will it be?" Don't make the employer think you're only in it for the money. The salary discussion should wait until later.

CHAPTER 11

Questions about Special Situations

DO YOU DREAD GOING ON JOB INTERVIEWS because you are afraid the interviewer will ask you about a situation you find embarrassing or one that you find difficult to explain? Were you fired from your last job or is there a huge gap in your work history? The interviewer is likely to notice any gaps or inconsistencies on your resume, so you need to be prepared for her to ask the questions you are most afraid of. Here are strategies for coping with that aspect of job interviewing.

I Hope They Don't Ask Me That

When a prospective employer reviews your resume, he will look for things like lengthy gaps between jobs or jobs that don't fit in with the rest of your experience. He will also notice if you hopped around from job to job or if a series of jobs don't move in an upward direction. An employer will probably question why you were at a job for a short period of time; he may also question why you have been with one employer for your entire career.

An interviewer may ask questions about your lack of experience if she feels you haven't been in the field long enough. If you appear to be overqualified for the job, the interviewer will question you about that as well. If you don't have the formal education that is called for, you will probably be asked to explain why. If your education is in one area and the job you are interviewing for is in another, the interviewer will inquire about that, too.

FACT

> An interviewer will also ask questions that aren't directly related to what he sees on your resume. While it gives the period of time you worked at each job, your resume doesn't show why you left each one. That is something the interviewer will try to ascertain. He may also ask about relationships between supervisors or coworkers that weren't exactly wonderful.

How to Answer Difficult Questions

When answering difficult questions, be honest and don't make excuses. The interviewer will appreciate your candor. It is preferable to lying or trying to cover up the truth. Many things can be learned through a thorough background check, so you are better off being up front. When possible, highlight the positive and talk about what you have done to overcome whatever it is that put a blemish on your past.

If an employer asks about a gap in employment, be honest about why it's there. Discuss things you did during that time to enhance your skills. For example, if you took time off to be at home with young children, talk about how you kept up with your career by reading and taking classes. If you didn't take up extra study during that time, talk about how you are preparing now for your return to work.

Address concerns about your lack of education or experience by explaining what you've done to compensate for it. If your experience makes up for your lack of a formal degree, say so. If you plan to take some courses to enhance your skills, talk about that. Remember to be specific.

If you were fired from a previous job, you may be concerned that revealing that information will take you out of the running for a job, but don't try to hide it. The prospective employer will probably want to talk to your prior boss before he hires you. When he does, he will learn the truth. Don't place blame on your employer or speak negatively about him.

 ESSENTIAL

You don't have to use the words *fired, terminated,* or *dismissed* to say you had to leave a job. All have negative connotations. *Laid off* sounds a little better, but may indicate that you were among many who were let go, which may not be accurate. You might want to say that you had a "parting of the ways" or a disagreement.

If you have been job-hunting for a while, you are probably concerned that a prospective employer will wonder why. Place blame on the economy if the current one is harsh. Even if the economy, in general, is good, the market for someone with your skills may not be. (Make sure the market really is bad first, though—you don't want to sound like you don't understand the industry.) State your skills and say that you haven't been able to find a job where those skills are needed.

Q. You were at your last job for only six months. Why so short a time?

A. Unfortunately, the job turned out to be much different than what I thought it would be. Fortunately though, I found this out early on—before the employer invested more time in me and I invested more time in the company. I know I could put my editing skills to much better use in this position.

Notice the interviewer places no blame on either herself or the employer. She doesn't say that the employer didn't tell her the truth about the job or that she misunderstood what she'd be doing. She also shows how she looked out for both her employer and herself by leaving before more time was invested.

 Never say: "My boss blatantly lied to me during the interview. The job turned out to be very different from what he told me." This candidate's mistake was speaking poorly of her former boss.

Ⓔ ALERT!

Keep your negativity in check. No matter how much you hate your former employer, keep your feelings to yourself.

Q. What do your subordinates think of you?

A. They think I'm a tough boss. I expect a lot out of them.

This answer provides just enough information to answer the question. She makes no indication of whether her subordinates like her or not.

Never say: "I'm a tough boss and because of that they resent me." This interviewee has said more than she needed to.

Q. I see from your resume that you've had five jobs in five years. Why have you moved around so much?

A. When I first graduated from college, I wasn't sure what I wanted to do. Five years later I'm committed to working in this field. I even took some courses to enhance my skills. I know I can do a good job here.

This is an honest answer. The candidate states that she is now committed to the field and proves it by talking about classes she has taken.

Never say: "I can't stay in one place for too long. . . . I mean, I couldn't stay in one place too long. Now I can." The candidate couldn't keep her answers straight, making the interviewer suspicious.

Q. You've been out of the job market for the last six years. Can you explain that, please?

A. I took a hiatus from the work force to raise my children. I am now ready to come back and use my skills. I have kept up with developments in the field during my absence by reading professional literature and attending seminars.

This candidate doesn't make excuses for her time away from the work force. She does make a point of letting the employer know that she didn't lose track of her career during this time.

Never say: "I was busy raising my family, but I can't afford to stay home anymore." This doesn't let the employer know that this candidate is ready to return to the work force, only that she has to.

Q. According to your resume, you were a manager at Crane Computer Store from 1990 through 1995 and then assistant manager at a different branch of the store starting in 1995. Were you demoted?

A. This wasn't a demotion. I was originally manager of the Paper Products Department. It was a very small section. When an opening came up for an assistant manager in the Home PC Department at another store, I jumped at the chance. It was a much better opportunity because it was a much larger department and I knew I would have greater responsibilities.

Although her job title would indicate this candidate had been demoted, she explains why this wasn't actually the case. She was willing to trade the "manager" title for a job with more responsibility. If she had been demoted, however, she would need to explain why.

Never say: "I didn't want all the responsibility of being a manager." Should this candidate really say that she doesn't want a job with responsibility?

Q. Why did you leave Community Publications Corporation?

A. My boss and I had a difference of opinion and we decided it would be best if I left my job.

The interviewee decides to be honest about his reasons for leaving his job. He doesn't blame his boss or berate himself, but simply tells the truth about being fired.

Never say: "That idiot fired me." Making disparaging comments about your boss is a poor choice.

Q. Tell me how your career progressed at your last job.

A. I was hired as assistant to the staff accountant. When she left, I was asked to take her position. After three months, my boss and I decided that I didn't yet have the skills for such a demanding job after all, and I stepped back into the assistant's position when they hired someone with more experience. That was three years ago, and I now have the experience I needed back then.

The candidate gives an honest answer. He explains that his "backward" progress from accountant to assistant was due to his lack of experience. He claims that he now has the experience to be a staff accountant.

Never say: "They promoted me before I was ready and then when they found someone they liked better, they sent me back to my original job." This answer makes the candidate sound very bitter about what happened. He also doesn't say anything about the skills he currently has.

Q. If I asked your previous supervisor for a reference, how would she describe you?

A. My supervisor and I often disagreed about many things. One thing we would agree on, I think, is that I do my job well.

This candidate is in a tricky situation. She and her supervisor don't get along, but that doesn't mean that she isn't a good employee. She gives this answer hoping that her former boss will put their differences aside and be honest about her performance at work if she is called as a reference.

Never say: "She probably has nothing nice to say. She's always had it in for me." This candidate doesn't give her a chance to say something bad about her—she does it herself.

Q. Your resume says that you are an administrative assistant, yet you're applying for a job that has much more responsibility. What makes you think you can handle it?

A. Even though my job title is administrative assistant, I have many more responsibilities than that title usually implies. I train all new support staff and supervise junior clerks.

This answer explains how this candidate's responsibilities differed from what one might assume from her job title. She chooses to discuss the aspects of her current job that are related to the job she is interviewing for.

Never say: "Even though I was technically an administrative assistant, I did a lot of other stuff." The candidate needs to explain what that "other stuff" was.

Q. You seem to be overqualified for this position. Why do you want this job?

A. I definitely bring a lot of skills to this job. I look forward to using my experience to help your company grow.

Rather than downplay her skills in response to what the interviewer has said, this candidate chooses to talk about how her experience and skills will benefit the company.

Never say: "I don't really have that much experience." A job candidate should never make less of her skills, regardless of what the interviewer thinks.

Q. There's a ten-year gap in your employment history. What were you doing during that time?

A. I was convicted of theft and was incarcerated at the state penitentiary from 1989 through 1999. During that time I earned a degree in social work that I want to use in working with young people who may be headed in the wrong direction.

A conviction will show up when the employer does a background check on this candidate, so it makes no sense for her to lie. She makes a point of discussing why she is qualified for the job she has applied for.

Never say: "I took some time off from the work force." The employer may hire the candidate in spite of a prior conviction, especially if she shows that she has turned her life around. If she lies about the conviction and the employer finds out the truth, she probably won't get the job.

Q. Have you ever been convicted of a felony?

A. Yes, I have. I served three years for a hit and run. I finished my college courses while I was in jail.

This candidate gives an honest answer and hopes it won't affect his chances of being hired. Generally, the interviewer can ask if a job candidate has ever been convicted of a felony.

Never say: "Why? Are you going to do a background check?" If he wasn't planning to do a background check, the employer will do one after hearing that response. Or he may simply decide to take this candidate out of consideration for the job.

Q. In your first job out of college you worked as a receptionist. Weren't you a little overqualified?

A. My education did overqualify me for that job, but I was determined to work in the advertising industry. I knew that if I took that job, it would give me the chance to show off my skills. I volunteered to do some proofreading for the copywriter, and after six months she asked me to be her assistant.

This candidate shows the interviewer that she knew what she had to do to reach her goals. She also tells the interviewer that her plan worked.

Never say: "It was the only thing available." This applicant did not have a clear goal in mind when she took the job.

Q. Your resume indicates that you've attended Harkin College, but I don't see a degree listed. Did you graduate?

A. No, I didn't graduate. I withdrew from the college during my junior year. I decided that I wasn't getting as much out of college as I should have, so I decided to go to work. I plan to continue my education in the future.

This is an honest answer. The candidate takes responsibility for discontinuing her formal education and expresses an interest in returning to school.

Never say: "The school was horrible. I didn't want to waste my parents' money." Couldn't the interviewee have attended a different school if this was the reason she dropped out?

Q. What were your grades like in college?

A. My grades could have been better. If I had it to do over again, I would have studied a lot harder than I did.

The candidate doesn't blame anyone but himself for his poor grades and makes a point of saying that he would do things differently now.

Never say: "They were okay." If the employer asks for a copy of this candidate's transcript, which he might, the candidate will be caught in a lie or the employer may question why his expectations were so low that he thought his poor grades were okay.

Q. If we hire you, the person who will be your supervisor is much younger than you are. Will this be a problem for you?

A. If she has the skills necessary to be a supervisor, I will be happy to work for her.

This candidate gives a straightforward answer to this question. She ignores the fact that the interviewer may be implying that she is too old for the job.

Never say: "Are you implying that I'm old?" The candidate is much too confrontational.

 FACT

In 2001, 10.3 percent of the labor force was between the ages of 55 and 64, and 3 percent were 65 or older. (U.S. Census Bureau, *Statistical Abstract of the United States: 2002.* Available from the World Wide Web: *www.census.gov*)

Q. It appears that you've been looking for work for about eight months. Can you explain that?

A. I am skilled in technical support, system design and implementation, and training. I haven't been able to find a position for someone with my skills.

This candidate gives an honest answer to the question. He states his skills and then explains that the job market has been tight for someone with those skills. Since he has no control over the job market, he doesn't have to make excuses for it.

Never say: "I know if I had looked harder for a job, I would have found one. After all, I have great skills." The candidate may think it's better to say he couldn't find a job because he wasn't looking for one, but this answer only shows his lack of motivation.

Q. Why are you applying for a job outside your major?

A. I know I can use the skills I developed as a psychology major to succeed in marketing research. I have taken courses in consumer behavior, statistics, and research design, which I know will be useful in this field.

This candidate shows how her skills are transferable to this field. She makes no mention of what her future plans are for staying in this field or going back to psychology.

Never say: "I need to work to save up money for graduate school." The employer has good reason to wonder how long this person will stay if he hires her.

Q. You don't seem to have a great deal of work experience. Why should we hire you?

A. I may not have a lot of paid work experience, but I have a lot of volunteer experience. I organized a voter registration drive in my community and registered 300 new voters during the last election. For the past four years I have chaired the committee that runs the book fair at my son's school. We have raised over $27,000.

While this candidate doesn't have paid work experience, she has been able to hone her skills through her volunteer work. She has persuaded people to register to vote and worked on a committee that successfully ran a major fundraising event. She even gives amounts to back up her claims.

Never say: "I really want this job, and I know I will be good at it." This candidate needs to talk about her skills.

Q. Aren't you underqualified for this job?

A. I don't think I am. I am willing to learn what I need to know to do the job.

The candidate doesn't try to explain her lack of experience. Instead she talks about getting the training she needs to do the job.

Never say: "I don't have a lot of experience, but how can I get any if no one will hire me?" Although what she is saying is true, this answer highlights the candidate's inexperience instead of addressing what she will do to change things.

Q. You've worked at the same company since you graduated from high school fifteen years ago. Why are you
looking for a new job now?

A. I learned a lot at my current job and I was given the opportunity to take on many different responsibilities. I decided to get
some formal training to enhance my skills in bookkeeping and
word processing. That training qualifies me for a job that requires
greater skills than my current one does.

*This candidate wants to use her new skills and therefore
must change jobs. This is reasonable and shows she is motivated to do the best that she can.*

Never say: "I'm bored." Many people leave their jobs because
they are bored. However, that's not a good way to impress a
prospective employer. The candidate should name something
specific about this new job that she is looking forward to.

Q. You're so young. What makes you think you can do
a good job?

A. I have a lot of experience in retail. I started working as a
retail clerk straight out of high school and over the last three years
I worked my way up to assistant manager.

*Rather than letting the interviewer lead her into a discussion
about her age, this candidate leads him into a discussion about
her experience.*

Never say: "What does my age have to do with it?" While it
is reasonable to have reservations about the interviewer's motives,
her approach is too confrontational.

Q. Your resume doesn't show any formal training in this field. What do you think qualifies you for this job?

A. While I don't have formal training in this field, I do have a lot of practical experience. As you can see from my resume, on my last job I spent a tremendous amount of time doing research. I plan to begin taking some courses so I can get my degree in this field.

This interviewee explains how her experience has given her the skills she needs to do this job. She also talks about her intention to get some formal training.

Never say: "I'm going to get my degree." While this answer shows that the candidate plans to develop her skills, it doesn't indicate that she currently has the skills necessary for this job.

Q. I see that all of your work experience has been in sales. What qualifies you to work in fundraising?

A. In sales I had to persuade people to buy our products. I was very good at it. I had the highest level of sales of anyone in my division. Now I would like to use my skills to sell people on this organization.

This candidate shows how he can transfer his sales skills to a career in fundraising.

Never say: "I think I will really like this field a lot more." This doesn't at all explain why he is qualified for the job.

Q. I noticed that your three previous jobs were in three different cities. Why did you move around so much?

A. My spouse was in the Marines, but he is retired now and working as a civilian in this city, so we're finally done moving around.

As a general rule, marital status should not be discussed on a job interview. However, the candidate must explain why he has moved around so much in the past and why he won't be doing that in the future.

Never say: "I won't be moving around a lot anymore." The interviewee can give a more elaborate answer than this one.

Q. You've been working outside the banking industry for the last year. Can you explain why you want to return now?

A. Yes, I can. The job market, as you know, has been bad for the last year and a half. It's been impossible for someone with my qualifications to find a job in the banking industry. In order to support my family, I had to take jobs in retail sales. I was happy to see your ad for a banking job that needs someone with my skills in branch management.

This candidate's only choice is to be honest. He is not to blame for the bad job market, so he makes no excuses for working outside his field for a year.

Never say: "I wanted to try out a new industry." It's okay to try out a new industry, but this candidate doesn't explain why he returned to the old one.

Q. I see you were manager at Wanda's Whispers. What type of business is that and what did you do there?

A. Wanda's Whispers is a retail store that sells women's lingerie. I was the store manager. I interviewed, hired, and trained the store's sales team.

Although she may be embarrassed to discuss the nature of the business, she proudly discusses her responsibilities there.

Never say: "The store sells ladies' apparel." The candidate is so flustered when she has to discuss this job that she neglects to discuss what she did there.

 ALERT!

> You may be embarrassed by the nature of a company that you worked for in the past. During the job interview you should focus on what your duties were and how they relate to the job you are interested in.

Q. You've been out of the work force for five years. Why re-enter it now?

A. I have a lot to offer. I've developed many skills over the last five years and I want to put them to use. I have excellent organization and time management skills. I am also great at resolving conflicts.

Rather than discussing what she hopes to get out of working, this candidate highlights what she can bring to a job.

Never say: "I'm in the process of getting divorced, so I have to go back to work." This is more information than anyone needs.

Q. I see you have a GED. Why did you drop out of high school?

A. I guess I was young and foolish then. It was a long time ago. I thought I didn't need school anymore, but I was sadly mistaken. I got my GED three years later and then went on to college. I'm looking forward to applying my training as a registered nurse to this position.

Youthful indiscretions can be forgiven. Although this candidate dropped out of high school, he did continue his education and is planning to move forward with his career.

Never say: "I don't remember. It was a long time ago." That isn't something one would easily forget. Since the candidate has gone on to complete his education, he shouldn't be ashamed to talk about his past.

Q. You didn't start working until two years after you got your degree. What were you doing?

A. I traveled extensively the year after I graduated from college. I backpacked across Europe for three months and then I spent four months in Australia. After that I traveled through the United States.

Had this candidate said that she sat at home watching television for a year after graduating, the interviewer would have assumed she was a little low on motivation. However, she explored the world, which was an admirable use of her time.

Never say: "I needed to take some time off. College was hard." Even if this candidate didn't have as interesting a story to tell as the previous candidate, she should have explained what she did during that time.

CHAPTER 12

Dealing With Illegal Questions

DO YOU KNOW WHICH QUESTIONS ARE ILLEGAL for an interviewer to ask? Many of the questions we consider illegal are not. Although there are some questions that are illegal, usually an employer is only breaking the law if she uses the answers to certain questions to discriminate against a candidate. Know what your rights are before going into an interview, and avoid answering questions that can illegally be used against you.

Who Decides What Questions Are Illegal?

The United States Congress has, over the years, passed federal laws that prohibit discrimination based on race, color, sex, national origin, religion, age, and disability. The U.S. Equal Employment Opportunity Commission (EEOC), an independent federal agency that was created by Congress in 1964, is charged with eradicating employment discrimination based on those federal laws. In order to do so, this agency interprets federal employment discrimination laws and coordinates all practices and procedures related to enforcing those laws. States, as well as local municipalities, also have laws against discrimination that sometimes cover more and are even stricter than the federal laws.

Most of these federal laws do not prohibit any questions outright, although state and local laws might. What they do is prohibit the employer from taking any information learned from asking certain questions and using it to discriminate against an applicant. So, if you are asked anything on an interview that you see listed in this chapter, don't go running to the EEOC just yet. However, if you get turned down for the job and you think it is because of your answer to one of these questions, you may have been the victim of discrimination.

When you think of illegal job interview questions, you may picture an employer being carted away in handcuffs for asking a prohibited question. That is an unlikely scenario. Even if the questions were illegal, or information obtained during an interview was used for discrimination, the job candidate would have to report the employer before any action would be taken and the result would be a lawsuit and possible fine, not jail time.

 ESSENTIAL

If you believe you have been discriminated against when applying for a job, you may file a charge of discrimination with the EEOC in person, by mail, or by telephone by contacting the nearest EEOC office. To find out where your local EEOC office is, call 1-800-669-4000 or 1-800-669-6820 (TTY). Visit *www.eeoc.gov* for more information.

The Rules Regarding Specific Issues

Each federal law that targets discriminatory hiring practices addresses a different issue. These are the main laws that specifically address discrimination in hiring:

- **Title VII of the Civil Rights Act of 1964** prohibits employment discrimination on the basis of race, color, religion, sex, or national origin.
- **The Age Discrimination in Employment Act of 1967** prohibits employment discrimination against individuals forty years of age and older.

- **Title I and Title V of the Americans with Disabilities Act (ADA) of 1990** prohibits employment discrimination on the basis of disability.

Following is a discussion of each issue covered by these laws. In addition, there are other laws on the books that prohibit discrimination in hiring due to marital status, sexual orientation, weight, and political affiliation. The National Labor Relations Act, which is enforced by the National Labor Relations Board, prohibits employers from asking job candidates if they are union members.

Race and Color Discrimination

According to Title VII of the Civil Rights Act of 1964, an employer cannot reject a job candidate based on the candidate's race or color. If an interviewer requests information that will disclose the candidate's race, the EEOC interprets that the information will be used as a basis for hiring. The request for that information would likely be used as evidence should the candidate bring charges of discrimination against the employer.

 ALERT!

An employer can ask for information on race if it is needed for affirmative action purposes, in which case it would have to be kept separately from the information that is used to make a hiring decision.

National Origin Discrimination

Title VII of the Civil Rights Act also keeps employers from discriminating against an individual because of his or her national origin. The interviewer may not ask you what country you or your parents are from. He may not ask you if you speak a foreign language unless it pertains to the duties of the job that you are interviewing for.

Religious Discrimination

An applicant, according to Title VII of the Civil Rights Act, cannot be discriminated against because of his religious beliefs. An employer cannot ask you what your religion is, if you belong to any religious groups, or if you go to a house of worship. She also cannot ask if your religious beliefs prevent you from working on certain days.

Pregnancy Discrimination

The Pregnancy Discrimination Act was passed in 1978 as an Amendment to Title VII of the Civil Rights Act. It states that as long as a woman is able to perform the major functions of her job, she cannot be passed over for employment because of a pregnancy-related condition. An interviewer cannot ask if you are pregnant or if you plan to become pregnant in the future.

Age Discrimination

The Age Discrimination in Employment Act of 1967 prohibits employment discrimination against individuals forty years of age and older. Some local laws prohibit age discrimination without specifying a minimum age. An interviewer may not ask you how old you are or when you graduated from high school or college, since providing that information would force you to reveal your age.

Discrimination Against the Disabled

The Americans with Disabilities Act (ADA), signed into law in 1990, prohibits an employer who has not yet made a job offer to a candidate from asking questions that are likely to reveal that candidate's disability. The employer must not ask questions about any health problems, such as a heart condition or asthma, or about mental illness. He cannot ask if you have a disability that would keep you from performing the job. Even if you have an obvious disability or if you reveal that you have a hidden one, the employer cannot ask you about it, with one exception. If the employer has good reason to believe that you will have difficulty performing a particular task, he can ask you if you will need "reasonable accommodation" to perform that task.

Q. How old are you?

A. I prefer to think of myself in terms of experience and not age. I have worked in this industry for quite some time. I have seen it go from a small playing field to what it is today. Fortunately I have kept up with all the changes by taking classes and constantly updating my skills.

Rather than address the issue of age, or the inappropriateness of this question, this candidate has instead decided to address some positive things about himself. He has a lot of experience and he strives to keep himself abreast of changes in the industry by taking classes.

Never say: "I'm fifty-two, but I look young for my age." This applicant should have avoided revealing his age.

Q. How much do you weigh?

A. My weight isn't an issue. I have never had a problem performing my job duties.

This question is not only rude, it may be illegal as well. This candidate explains how her weight doesn't affect her ability to do her job.

Never say: "I'm thinking of getting my stomach stapled." Although she has asked a rude question, the employer has learned that this candidate might need some time off from work, and she hasn't even started yet.

Q. What is your race?

A. I'm African-American and Asian.

If an employer asks a question about race, his intentions are usually not good, so make a mental note that you were asked. If the employer discriminates against you based on your race, the information you provided in this answer can be used as evidence against him if you file a complaint with the EEOC.

Never say: "That is an illegal question. You can't ask me that." You are certainly within your rights to take an interviewer to task for asking such an inappropriate question, but the question in itself isn't illegal unless the information garnered from it is used to discriminate against you.

Q. Were you born in the United States?

A. I'm not sure why you're asking me that. Can you explain?

This question is inappropriate and the employer probably knows that. The candidate gives him a chance to correct himself. Perhaps all the employer needs to know is that the candidate is eligible to work in the United States.

Never say: "I came here from Poland two years ago." The candidate is not required to reveal that information.

Q. Where were your parents born?

A. My parents came to this country thirty years ago. They worked very hard to put me through school and are very proud of my successful career. They passed their work ethic down to me.

This candidate chooses not to reveal his national origin and instead manages to talk about his own qualities. There is nothing that says a candidate shouldn't reveal his national origin, just that he doesn't have to.

Never say: "My parents are from Greece and Portugal." This candidate is giving out more information than is necessary.

Q. Your last name sounds Spanish. Is it?

A. Yes, it is.

The applicant has a choice to make. She can refuse to answer or she can just give a simple answer, as she did. If this was the only question of this type, the interviewer may have just been trying to make conversation.

Never say: "My father was born in Guatemala. My mother was born in Ireland." This candidate reveals more about her national origin than she needs to.

 ALERT!

You should always make a point of sounding confident when answering questions on a job interview. If you sound unsure of yourself, the interviewer will pick up on it.

Q. What is your sexual orientation?

A. I don't think that has anything to do with this job.

Sexual orientation isn't something that should be discussed on a job interview.

 Never say: "I'm gay" or "I'm straight." While employers might be prohibited from discriminating based on sexual orientation, this information isn't relevant to the job interview.

Ⓔ FACT

Federal law currently does not protect job candidates from employment discrimination based on their sexual orientation. However, many state and local laws do. There are thirteen states that currently protect gay men and lesbians from employment discrimination.

Q. How tall are you?

A. I'm five foot seven.

Although an employer shouldn't ask an applicant about any physical characteristics, including height and weight, answering it shouldn't cause a problem.

 Never say: "You can't ask me that." While that is true, that response may unnecessarily cause hard feelings, especially if the interviewer meant no harm in asking it.

Q. What is your religious background?

A. I consider religion a very personal thing, so I would rather not discuss it.

***

The applicant can always choose to politely refuse to answer a question she considers improper. That is what she decides to do.

✗ Never say: "How dare you ask me that?" While the candidate can refuse to answer the question, there is no reason to be that confrontational.

Q. Will your religion keep you from working on Saturday or Sunday?

A. Perhaps we can discuss the details of my schedule after we both confirm that I'm the right candidate for this position.

***

This candidate knows Title VII of the Civil Rights Act requires that an employer reasonably accommodate the religious practices of an employee or applicant as long as doing so doesn't pose a hardship. He also knows that an employer cannot decide to reject a candidate based on the knowledge that this accommodation will be necessary. However, he chooses to wait until he receives an offer before discussing this.

✗ Never say: "I can't work on Saturday." Although the employer can't make a decision based on this information, it isn't necessary to discuss it at this point.

Q. Do you have any children?

A. I understand that you may be concerned that having a family might get in the way of someone's career. However, that has never been the case with me. I'm very dedicated to my career.

Without giving a direct answer to this question, the candidate has chosen to reassure the employer that having a family, or not having one, will not influence her career.

Never say: "I don't have children yet." If the employer chooses not to hire this candidate, it may be because this answer indicates she might have children in the future. Whether or not this constitutes discrimination might be vague, since she doesn't currently have children.

Ⓔ ESSENTIAL

When faced with an improper question about your family or marital status, you can choose to address the issue head-on. You can reassure the interviewer that having a family has not, and will not, interfere with your career.

Q. Are you planning to have children?

A. I am very committed to my career. Whether or not I have children will not affect that.

This interviewee tells the employer the only thing he has the right to know—that she is dedicated to her career.

Never say: "I've always wanted to have children." The candidate did not have to answer this question.

Q. What child care arrangements do you have in place?

A. I'm sensing that you may have concerns about scheduling. I have a great attendance record on my current job. I haven't missed a day of work in two years.

This candidate has decided to address the intent of the interviewer's question. Since she believes he is afraid that child care problems will cause her to miss work, she informs him of her perfect attendance record.

Never say: "My child goes to day care." The employer is out of line in asking this question. However, this candidate's answer only heightens his concern since a child will not be able to go to day care when he is ill. That means Mom (or Dad) will have to miss work.

Q. Are you married?

A. No, I'm not.

Although this question is inappropriate and may be illegal, depending on where you live, the candidate sees no harm in answering it.

Never say: "I'm getting married in six months and let's see . . . sixteen days." This answer implies that the interviewee is very immersed in his wedding plans and perhaps may not be able to give the necessary attention to his job.

Q. Do you belong to a union?

A. Will I be required to join a union?

The NLRA prohibits employers from questioning applicants about their union sympathies. This candidate chooses to avoid the question by asking her own.

Never say: "Yes." The employer can't make a decision based on this information, and wasn't legally allowed to ask it in the first place. The candidate certainly didn't have to answer it.

Q. Are you a Democrat or Republican?

A. I've always felt that it's a bad idea to discuss religion or politics with anyone. Therefore, I'm going to refrain from answering that question.

The candidate has given a polite answer, but has refused to provide the information the interviewer improperly requested.

Never say: "I'm a Democrat (or Republican)." Your political affiliation has nothing to do with how well you perform on the job. There is no reason an interviewer needs to know this.

 FACT

> The EEOC does not enforce laws that prohibit discrimination based on a person's political affiliation. However, other federal agencies and many states and municipalities do enforce such laws. For assistance contact the EEOC office nearest you.

Q. Will your spouse mind the long hours you will have to work here?

A. I've always worked very long hours, so this won't be a problem.

***

This candidate chooses to address the question about the long hours he will be required to work.

Never say: "My wife would love me to get a job with fewer hours, but there aren't many like that out there." There is no reason to give this much information. The interviewee's answer will set off some alarms. Since his wife is unhappy with his hours, if a job with fewer hours came along, he would take it.

Q. How do you want to be addressed? Miss or Mrs.?

A. You can just call me Robin.

***

The interviewer is trying to ascertain the candidate's marital status, but she won't play into it. She dodges the issue altogether.

Never say: "I prefer Mrs. Brown." The candidate could have avoided letting the interviewer know her marital status.

Ⓔ ESSENTIAL

When an interviewer asks you an improper question, you can refuse to answer it, you can confront the interviewer, or you can answer it. Information you give voluntarily can be used against the employer if he discriminates.

Q. Have you ever been arrested or convicted of a crime?

A. No. I have never been convicted of a crime.

An employer may not ask you if you have ever been arrested but you can be legally asked if you've been convicted of a crime. Notice how this candidate avoids the arrest question. She doesn't want to lie or discuss an arrest that she was not convicted for.

 Never say: "I was arrested once but I wasn't convicted." Since the employer may only ask about prior convictions, the applicant didn't have to talk about her arrest at all.

Q. Have you ever committed a crime?

A. If you're asking if I've ever been convicted of a crime, no I haven't.

An employer may ask if an applicant has been convicted of a crime, but he may not ask if he has committed one or if he has been arrested.

Never say: "Yes, but I was never convicted." The candidate didn't have to reveal this fact.

Ⓔ QUESTION?

What should I do if I was in jail?
If you were convicted of a felony, this information will be revealed in a background check. You might as well be up front about it.

Q. I see you're limping. Did you hurt yourself?

A. I'm fine, thank you.

The employer, according to ADA, cannot inquire about an applicant's injury and the candidate is under no obligation to reveal it.

 Never say: "I have cerebral palsy." The candidate is not required to reveal any information regarding his disability.

Ⓔ FACT

> The Americans With Disabilities Act allows an employer to ask a job candidate whether she will need accommodations to do the job if hired, but only if the candidate has an obvious disability and it is reasonable to believe she will need accommodations to do the job. The employer cannot ask about the nature of the disability.

Q. Do you have a heart condition?

A. With all due respect, I don't have to answer that question.

The applicant has a right to refuse to answer this question. The ADA makes questions about one's health illegal.

Never say: "Yes, I do." The employer is legally prohibited from asking this question and the candidate does not have to answer it.

Q. Will you need us to make any accommodations in order for you to do your job?

A. I am able to perform all functions of the job as you described it.

ADA prohibits the employer from asking this question, even if she asks it of all applicants. The only reason an employer may ask this question is if the applicant's disability is obvious and the employer has good reason to believe she will need accommodation.

Never say: "Yes, I will." The applicant doesn't have to answer this question unless her disability is obvious. In that case she can explain what accommodations she will need.

Q. Have you ever been treated for mental health problems?

A. I have, but everything is under control now. I have always performed well at work and I know I will continue to.

Although he is under no obligation to reveal this information at any time, this candidate knows he may need reasonable accommodation in the future.

Never say: "No, I haven't" if you have. This candidate just lied to his prospective employer. Although he is within his legal rights to withhold information regarding his mental health, he has to consider whether he plans to reveal this information at a later date and what the consequences may be if he does. Although the employer can't fire an employee because of the employee's mental illness, he may distrust him for lying, which will damage their relationship. He would be better off telling the truth, or simply saying he'd rather not discuss it.

Q. Have you ever been treated for drug addiction?

A. That was some time ago and I prefer not to discuss it.

This candidate is within her rights not to discuss this. Those who have been treated for drug addiction are covered by the ADA, and a hiring decision cannot be based upon this.

 Never say: "Yes, and I've only slipped up twice since then." The ADA doesn't protect someone who is currently using drugs from discrimination.

ⓔ FACT

An employer can refuse to hire someone who currently uses illegal drugs. The ADA does not protect the applicant in this case. In addition, tests for illegal drugs are not subject to the ADA's restrictions on medical examinations.

Q. Do you currently take any prescription drugs?

A. I've taken medication from time to time but it has never had an effect on my work.

This answer does not reveal whether the candidate is currently taking medication, and by law she doesn't have to reveal that.

Never say: "Yes, I take pain medication." There is no reason the candidate needed to reveal that information.

Q. How many days were you sick last year?

A. I would have to check with my former employer and get back to you.

This question is illegal following the guidelines set forth by the ADA. The candidate has chosen to avoid answering it.

Never say: "I had a heart attack last year and I missed a month of work." The candidate was under no obligation to answer this question.

Q. Travel is a big part of this job. Will your family be okay with that?

A. I can assure you that traveling will not be a problem. I traveled extensively on my previous job.

This candidate has chosen to let the employer know that her family status will not affect her job. She mentions the fact that her previous job had similar requirements and it wasn't a problem.

Never say: "Traveling shouldn't be a problem. I just have to make sure my husband and I aren't out of town at the same time." By giving this answer, the candidate acknowledges that traveling could be a problem.

 ESSENTIAL

> When discussing what you would do if you were hired, you should draw on your past experience. Talk about how you completed similar projects on your last job or how you made similar decisions.

Q. You're a young single guy living in the city. How do you handle having women chase after you?

A. Work has always been my priority.

It is inappropriate for the employer to ask a question regarding the applicant's sex life. The candidate chooses to evade the question by talking about work.

Never say: "Can you believe I'm dating five different women right now?" This candidate has chosen to answer a question he didn't have to, and in doing so may cause the employer to wonder how he will have any time for work.

Q. Whom should we notify in case of an emergency?

A. I have to give it some thought. Can I let you know?

The employer does not need this information before the employee begins to work for her. This may be a thinly disguised attempt to learn about the candidate's personal life; that is, what her marital status is.

Never say: "You can notify my husband. His name is . . ." This answer reveals information about the candidate's personal life.

CHAPTER 13

Behavioral Interviews

THROUGHOUT A JOB INTERVIEW you will be given many opportunities to tell an employer about yourself. So far you've learned how to talk about many things, including your personality, skills, work experience, and educational background. You've even learned what to do if you are asked improper or illegal questions. Now it's time to talk about behavioral questions. These will give you the chance to really show off your qualifications by giving the employer clear examples of what you can do.

What Are Behavioral Interview Questions?

When an employer conducts interviews, his primary goal is to make sure the person he hires can do the job. "Doing the job" involves using your knowledge, skills, and abilities in combinations referred to as competencies. In addition to your knowledge and skills in your particular occupational field, your competencies include:

- Decision-making
- Time management
- Problem solving
- Organization
- Multitasking
- Interpersonal skills

- Writing and presentation skills
- Team building
- Flexibility

In a behavioral interview, you will be asked for specific real-life examples of situations that illustrate whether or not you have the skills and abilities necessary to do the job by explaining how you have used them in the past. These questions that focus on specific situations are called behavioral interview questions.

 FACT

You may be faced with a behavioral interview, a standalone entity where you are asked only behaviorally oriented questions, or it may be incorporated into your regular interview with only some of the questions behavioral in nature.

Why Employers Ask Behavioral Questions

If you ever want to know how a person will react to something in the future, find out how they reacted to something similar in the past. That is why employers use behavioral interviews. Knowing what you did in the past allows them to predict what you will do in the future.

Before she begins interviewing candidates, the employer will determine what competencies the person she hires must have. During the interview, she will listen carefully to your answers to determine whether you have those particular competencies.

Of course, the employer can ask you whether you have a particular competency, but wouldn't it be better if she could get you to demonstrate it? That is where behavioral interview questions come in. The employer will use behavioral interview questions to get you to demonstrate your competencies by discussing a situation when you used them.

How to Answer Behavioral Questions

When answering behavioral questions, your goal is to show the employer why you are the best candidate for the job. You must demonstrate that you have the competencies he is seeking. Behavioral questions require the most preparation of any you will be asked on a job interview.

If you know what competencies the employer needs, you will have an easier job preparing for the interview. These competencies may be detailed in a job description. Consider yourself lucky if they are. If not, you will have to dig a little to try to make some prediction. Do some research to find out what knowledge, skills, and abilities in particular this company values.

 ESSENTIAL

Your research prior to a job interview will help you answer many of the questions the interviewer will ask you. Use your network to find people who may have experience with that employer. The more you can find out about a company, the better you will understand the qualities it is looking for in an employee.

Once you know what competencies the employer needs you to have, you have to come up with some anecdotes that highlight those competencies. Choose those that are from your work history, or your school experiences if you are a recent graduate. Select anecdotes that are truthful and show you in the best light possible.

When answering a behavioral question, you should first present the task or problem that you faced. Then you should explain what steps you took to accomplish the task or solve the problem, making sure to highlight the competencies you used. Next you should talk about the results you achieved.

Q. Tell me about something you've done to motivate your coworkers.

A. About a year ago our company went through some tough times and about twenty-five workers were laid off. Morale was lower than I had ever seen it. This happened right around the time we had to start putting together our holiday issue, and no one was really into it. I planned a "winter in July" party to pick up everyone's spirits and to get us ready to work on the magazine. By the time the party was over, we were all in a better mood and ready to put together a great issue. I think it was one of the best ones we ever did.

The job candidate has demonstrated that he knows how to motivate others.

Q. What is the toughest group that you have had to get cooperation from?

A. I was asked to teach a new procedure to the customer service team. I had heard rumblings to the effect that many people on the team were unhappy with the new procedures, so I knew I wasn't going to have a receptive group to work with. Before I could be effective at teaching them what they needed to know, I had to convince them that the new procedure would benefit them. So, I set up a presentation that explained how it would save them time. Once the team saw the benefits of the new procedure, they actually looked forward to the training. They learned very quickly and we were able to implement the procedure in less than a week.

The interviewee demonstrates two competencies in her response. She highlights her interpersonal skills when she talks about how she was aware of the customer service team's concerns. Then she highlights her presentation skills.

Q. Describe a situation in which you had a positive influence on someone else's actions.

A. One of the new guys in my department was assigned a couple of projects at once and couldn't figure out how he would get both of them done on time. He was really frantic since he had only been there for a short time and was approaching his first performance evaluation. He knew only too well that these projects were crucial to his getting a good evaluation. When he told me about his concerns, I asked him how he was scheduling his work and whether he was setting deadlines for completing different portions of his project. He had no idea what I was talking about. This was his first real job and this is something they don't teach you in school. I spent a lunch hour teaching him how to set up work schedules. After we met he set up work schedules for both projects and asked me to look them over. I did and helped him make a couple of changes. He completed both projects by their deadlines and got a pretty good performance evaluation.

In describing how he helped his colleague, this candidate shows that he has good interpersonal skills. He also manages to demonstrate his own time management skills by describing how he taught his coworker to set a schedule for himself.

 FACT

In today's workplace, most people work on teams. A team must function as a single entity whose goal is to complete a project efficiently. Members of teams must appreciate one another's differences and be willing to compromise.

Q. Can you demonstrate how you have been effective with your organization and planning?

A. A few months ago I was assigned a big project. The chairperson of my department asked me to assemble a committee, made up of faculty and students, to evaluate the current curriculum. She gave us two semesters to complete the project.

The first thing I had to do was decide who to include on the committee. I chose a few members of the faculty who had been with us for a very long time, as well as some who recently joined the department. The students I picked ranged from freshmen to graduate students. I wanted a wide cross-section of both faculty and students. After that I set up deadlines for certain parts of the project to be completed and I set up a schedule for meetings. Finally, each person was assigned a specific area to look at and then present for discussion at each meeting.

Based on the work of this committee, we were able to drop some courses that were not effectively meeting the goals of the department. We were able to add other courses that were innovative and would attract students.

By giving this answer, the candidate demonstrates that she is good at organizing and planning projects.

 ALERT!

If you can't draw upon your experience to answer a question, don't make something up. You can use a hypothetical situation as an example, but let the interviewer know you are doing that.

Q. Have you ever been a member of a group where some of the members did not work well together? Describe what you did.

A. Yes, I have. I was a member of a group that was developing a new software program for kids. There were three of us on the team. I got along with the two people that I was working with, but they didn't get along with each other at all. They constantly shot down each other's ideas and they expected me to take sides. I refused to do that. Instead I tried to help them see each other's point of view. I explained how they each had good ideas and helped them compromise. In the end we had a very successful product.

With this answer, the job candidate demonstrates that he has good interpersonal skills and good team-building skills.

Q. Give an example of a time when you went above and beyond the call of duty.

A. I've been teaching algebra for seven years and I know some children really have difficulty understanding it. There's only so much individual attention I can give to each student during class, so any help I give them has to be at another time. I teach five classes a day, which leaves only two free periods. One is a prep period and one is my lunchtime. I decided the kids needed math help more than I needed lunch, so I set aside three times a week when they could come to my room for tutoring. Many students have taken me up on this extra help and their grades have improved significantly. Most of my students do really well on the statewide seventh-grade test as a result of my tutoring them.

This candidate demonstrates that she is a compassionate teacher who makes time for her students.

Q. Describe a time when you were assigned several projects at the same time.

A. That happens very often, but one time that stands out in my mind is last year during the fall. The managers of three departments, women's outerwear, toys, and women's accessories asked me to set up their winter holiday displays. They all wanted them up within a week. I knew there was no way I could complete all three in one week.

Since I know customers are more likely to shop for kids' presents first, and kids really enjoy the displays, I decided to decorate the toy department first. I checked with the other two managers to see if they had some flexibility in their scheduling and both did. I scheduled both departments to have their displays up the following week.

All three departments were beautifully decorated for the holidays and I completed them in two weeks.

This interviewee demonstrates knowledge about her industry when she discusses why she chose to decorate the toy department first. She goes on to show how she is good at planning and scheduling.

 FACT

The ability to prioritize is highly valued in today's fast-paced workplace. An employee must also be able to multitask and manage her time well. She must also be highly organized.

Q. Can you give an example of how you adjust to unforeseen circumstances?

A. Last summer I was one week away from a big presentation. All of a sudden the power went out. We soon found out the lights were out everywhere in the East. Fortunately I was two days ahead of schedule, but we didn't know when power would be restored. I was worried I wouldn't be able to work on my presentation, which could end up making the company look bad and could cost us a lot of money. Our battery backup was still working, so I decided to print out the presentation so I could work by hand if necessary. I wrote a lot of the presentation by hand that day. All I had left to do were my slides, which I did when the power came back on the next afternoon.

The job candidate shows that he knows how to cope with an emergency.

Q. Give an example of a quick decision you made.

A. When we were working on our April issue last year, one of the designers we planned to feature backed out just before the photo shoot because she didn't feel her line was ready. We had planned to feature her work on about twenty pages. Now we had to figure out what to do with those pages. We didn't have much time to waste. The photographer was on his way and was going to get paid for a day's work whether we used him or not. It turned out one of my assistant editors knew an up-and-coming designer. I decided to take a chance on the new designer since I trusted my assistant's opinion. The shoot was wonderful and her designs were fantastic. The issue was great and we've featured that designer a few times since then.

This interviewee shows that she knows how to make quick decisions.

Q. Describe how you multitask.

A. Since I work for three lawyers, I regularly have to multitask. Just two weeks ago they walked into my office one after another, handed me files, and told me they needed the work in them completed by the end of the week. I looked at the files and I figured out how long each assignment would take. Then I looked to see if there was any overlap between the assignments. I discovered that each required some research, which I was able to do that afternoon. The next morning I began working on the first project. I needed some files to do the other two projects, so I asked one of the file clerks to retrieve those for me while I put the finishing touches on the first assignment. With those files in front of me, I was able to work on the other two assignments.

In explaining her ability to multitask, this candidate highlights her project-planning skills, and her ability to delegate some work to others.

Q. Give me an example of when you showed initiative and took the lead.

A. A year ago we noticed that our students' grades on statewide language arts exams were slipping. I had recently attended a seminar that addressed this particular issue and ways to resolve it. I had a program in mind that I thought we could implement at our school. I spoke to my principal about it and he asked me to write a formal proposal. After I did that and he approved it, I put together a committee of teachers and parents who would work with me to implement the program. This year's exam, as you know, won't take place until next month, but I think we'll see big improvements.

By giving this answer, the candidate shows how she recognized a problem and took initiative in resolving it.

Q. Describe a written report you had to complete.

A. My boss asked me to develop a plan to improve our quality-control process. He gave me a month to come up with three different ideas and said he would choose the best one based on my report.

The first thing I noticed was that we didn't have a written document that described the procedure we were currently using, so I had to put one together. Then I began to research quality-control processes used by other companies. The librarian at our local library was able to tell me what databases I could access to find articles that discussed this issue. Through my research I was able to find which quality-control processes were most successful. I chose the three that I thought would work best for my employer and wrote about them. The report included my recommendation as to which one I thought we should use.

My boss was pleased with the report. He agreed with my recommendation and my next project involved implementing the new process, including writing a document that described it completely.

This answer demonstrates this candidate's ability to put together a written report, including using research skills.

 ESSENTIAL

Certain soft skills are vital to one's performance at work. Without these skills, the employee simply can't do his job. Make a point of demonstrating that you have these skills, which include multitasking, organizing, time management, and decision-making.

Q. Give me an example of how you dealt with a conflict between two of your employees.

A. A year ago two of my employees started having problems getting along with each other. It came from out of the blue but looked like it had the potential to escalate rapidly. I called separate meetings with each of the employees. Remarkably they had similar stories and one did not really blame the other for what had happened. They agreed on a joint meeting, where I was able to help them realize that they really were on the same page after all. Things between them are now back to the way they were. They are both productive members of my department, so I'm glad we were able to work things out.

This candidate demonstrates her skill in conflict resolution.

Q. Describe a recent unpopular decision you made and what the result was.

A. A few months ago we found that we were having difficulty scheduling people to cover the circulation desk during lunch hours. Almost everyone wanted to go to lunch at 1 P.M., which meant we wouldn't have enough people around to check books in and out for our patrons. I decided that the only way to deal with this was to schedule lunch hours. We had two lunch hours—12 to 1 P.M. or 1 to 2 P.M. Staff could go to lunch only at the time they were assigned. No one liked this idea very much because they were used to going to lunch whenever they felt like it. Something had to be done, however, because if we didn't do something service would suffer. Scheduled lunch hours have been in effect for the past three months. The staff have gotten used to it and service has definitely improved.

The interviewer shows that she is a good manager who isn't afraid to make decisions that may be unpopular.

Q. Have you ever had to deal with someone with whom you had a bad working relationship? Describe what you did.

A. My boss asked me to work on a project with the one person in my company I don't get along with. We both possess unique skills that were required for that particular project. I knew we'd be working together for several months and I didn't want those months to be miserable. I decided to swallow my pride and invite my coworker to lunch. We discussed the project and what we would have to do to make it work. We both realized that the company would be the victim if we let our personal differences get in the way of our performance. We divided the project up so that we could each work independently using our individual strengths, but we wound up working together more than we expected, so we learned to appreciate each other's strengths and how to use them in combination to benefit the company. We completed the project and we've worked on several other ones together since then. Even though we still don't always agree on things, we know how to work well together now.

The candidate demonstrates how she used her interpersonal skills to resolve her differences with her coworker.

 FACT

When an employer hires someone, she is investing in that person's future as an employee. A poor hiring decision means that investment is wasted. That is why employers take job interviewing very seriously.

Q. Tell me about a recent situation in which you had to deal with a very upset customer.

A. Just last week one of our customers called, extremely upset because something we had shipped to her had arrived damaged. One of her customers was coming in to pick up the item two days later and she didn't want to disappoint her. I assured her that she would have the item for her customer on time. I brought the merchandise to the shipping department myself and asked that it be sent out by overnight delivery.

She called the next day to say that her package had arrived. She thanked us for resolving this quickly and placed another order.

The candidate has demonstrated that she has good interpersonal skills.

Q. Tell me about the most difficult person you've ever had to work with.

A. That would have to be Jen. Jen was a perfectly nice person but she liked giving her work to others. She didn't have the right to do that. Our supervisor was the one who assigned work to us and he expected each of us to handle that work on our own.

One day I decided I had had enough of this. Jen asked me to make some phone calls for her, and I told her we needed to have a talk. We did, and it turned out that Jen was overwhelmed by all the work our boss assigned and she didn't know how to handle it, other than getting help from her coworkers. I helped her figure out a way to manage her time better and get her work done on her own. Jen is doing a lot better now. She doesn't try to pass off her work to other people anymore.

This candidate shows that she has good interpersonal skills and is willing to help others succeed.

Q. Describe a situation in which you were able to effectively "read" another person and guide your actions based on what you understood about his or her needs and values.

A. About eight months ago, a client approached us about a new product they were introducing. There were two people I could have assigned to work on that project. Both would have done a good job—they are equally skilled and had worked with the client before. Knowing what I know about one of those employees, I had a feeling this new product was contrary to some of her personal values.

I didn't want to jump to any conclusions, so I spoke to her before I made a decision about this. I was correct. She would have worked on the project, but she wouldn't have been comfortable with it. I decided to assign it to the other person.

The client was very happy with the way things went. The product was introduced over the summer and has been very successful. They've had sales of about $1.5 million.

This candidate demonstrates her interpersonal skills by giving this answer.

 ESSENTIAL

Your impulsive nature may be admired when you're hanging out with your friends. However, at work your boss expects you to think through all your decisions carefully. Your response to questions on your interview should in no way reveal that you are impulsive.

Q. Have you ever anticipated a problem while working on a project and found a way to avoid it?

A.While working on a project in October, I realized that the person who had done the budget hadn't included printing costs. It wasn't going to be a huge expense, but it was definitely something that needed to be included in the budget.

First I figured out what the cost of printing would be. Then I looked at the rest of the budget to see if the other costs were accurate. I found a few places where the costs had been over-stated a little bit. I was able to change some numbers around so the money allotted for those expenses could instead be used for printing. We were still a little short, so I had to talk to my boss about increasing the budget. He was able to do that because the amount we needed wasn't very significant.

Not only does this candidate demonstrate that she can antic-ipate and avoid problems, she also shows that she knows how to budget expenses.

 ALERT!

Your goals should always be aligned with those of the employer. If the employer senses that your goals have nothing to do with your prospective job, you probably won't be working for her anytime soon. Goals like cutting costs and increasing productivity are always appreciated.

Q. Have you ever found working on a team disappointing? Did you do anything that helped things improve?

A. In a business course I took in college, we were assigned to teams to work on a project that involved running a "company." At the beginning we had trouble working together. However, we were being graded as a group, so we had to find a way to use our differences rather than let them defeat us. I thought the project would be more successful if we drew on every member's strengths and interests. Once I explained this to everyone, we redivided the tasks. We used our different strengths and interests to put together a successful project and got an A.

The interviewee takes this opportunity to demonstrate her team-building skills as well as her leadership skills.

Q. Tell me about a problem you solved.

A. I was coordinating a trade show in Washington, DC. We advertised in all the industry publications and got an unprecedented number of responses from vendors who wanted to display their products. There were 350 companies that wanted to reserve booths. I knew our current venue had insufficient space. We could have turned away some of the vendors, but since they represent a significant amount of revenue, I didn't think this was even an option. I started looking into larger venues. I thought the new Washington Convention Center would be perfect. There was plenty of room to accommodate everyone, and with the extra participation we were able to afford the larger site. We went ahead and booked it. The trade show was very successful. Both attendees and vendors were thrilled with the event. Many expressed an interest in attending next year.

The interviewer demonstrates her problem-solving skills.

Q. Tell me about a time when you had to use your presentation skills to influence a client.

A. My former employer had one particular client who had to be convinced that our way was the best way to go every time we made a presentation. He always needed a lot of reassurance, which was his right since he was paying good money for our services. There was one particular project I worked on for him where he needed even more convincing than usual. He wanted to redesign the packaging for one of his hair-care products. We put together a package design that was unique—the bottle was oval shaped instead of the usual cylindrical shape. It would really stand out from everything else on the shelves. Since it was an unconventional design and he was pretty conservative, he was hesitant to proceed.

I asked our research department to put together some focus groups. The response to the design was very positive. Ninety percent of those we surveyed said they liked the new design better than the old one, and 85 percent picked that product from a group of three other similar products. We presented that information to the client and sold him on the oval shape. He went ahead with it and saw a 22 percent increase in sales in the first six months after the new design was introduced.

This interviewee demonstrates what he is asked to. He has the presentation skills necessary to influence his client's decision.

 FACT

You should always try to quantify your answer using actual numbers. When you talk about raising money, increasing sales, or cutting costs use actual figures to back up your claim.

Q. Tell me how you delegate work effectively.

A. One of our clients asked us to work on a major project for them. It involved a conference they were holding in six months. They expected thousands of people to attend and they needed us to help them choose a location, get the best rates on hotels, find caterers, and then organize the event. I picked three people on my staff to work on this project with me. One person had a lot of experience in travel, so I asked her to choose the location and work with some hotels in the area to get us the best rates for those who were attending the conference. Another person had worked on an event for a different client and she had done a great job choosing the caterer, so I asked her to arrange for the meals and refreshments. Finally, I picked the most organized person on my staff to collect responses from those who signed up for the conference. He had to assign them to tables for meals and had to figure out who would attend which conference events.

I have to say my staff did a great job. I was so proud of them. Over 5,000 people attended the conference and all went well.

This candidate shows how she used her delegation skills to successfully complete an assignment.

 ALERT!

Never lie on a job interview and say you have experience you don't have. The chance of getting caught in a lie is too great. If you can find some related experience, talk about that and explain how it is similar.

Q. Give me an example of a time when you used your fact-finding skills to solve a problem.

A. I was advisor to a student who needed to request a leave of absence from the university. I didn't know what the proper procedures were to officially do this. I didn't want to have her do it incorrectly and then be inadvertently dropped from the program. I asked our department secretary if there was a written document that discussed the procedure. He didn't know of one. I then contacted the registrar's office. They referred me to the associate dean's office. I finally got the answer there and was able to tell the student what she needed to do.

The candidate, as asked, demonstrates how he has used his fact-finding skills.

Q. Tell me about a time when you had to make an unpopular decision.

A. As director of our after-school program, I noticed that parents were often arriving very late to pick up their children. That meant that staff had to stay late too, which meant we had to pay them for their time. We simply didn't have the money to do that. I decided we would have to charge parents if they were late in order to have the money to pay our staff. Many people weren't happy with this, but we really didn't have a choice.

This was enough incentive to get parents to pick up their children on time. As a matter of fact, late pickups decreased by 85 percent right after this program went into effect.

This answer demonstrates that the candidate is willing to make an unpopular decision in order to solve a problem.

Q. Tell me about a project you initiated.

A. Last February, my boss took a three-week vacation. He left me some work to do while he was gone, but I finished it by the end of the first week. I had wanted to reorganize our files for a long time, and now I had the time to work on this. First I developed a plan to work on the project. I set up a schedule that included setting goals for what I wanted to complete by the end of each day in order to finish within two weeks. Then I figured out what filing system I wanted to use. I recruited our intern to help me. We finished the project on the Friday my boss was set to return. He was happy to see what I had done while he was gone.

This answer demonstrates several competencies. The candidate takes initiative when she takes on a project without being asked. She shows that she knows how to plan and schedule a project and also how to delegate tasks.

Q. Describe a big presentation you had to deliver.

A. I had to make a big presentation at a national trade show. I was standing in for my supervisor who had to be somewhere else that day. He gave me the assignment two weeks before the show, so I had to prepare the presentation within a pretty tight time frame. First I set goals for completing each part of the presentation. Then I scheduled meetings with the developers of the products I'd have to present at the show so I could make sure I knew everything I could about them. I put together a great presentation. We took orders from 150 retailers that day alone and the sales on the products I presented increased by 15 percent after the show.

The candidate highlights her time management skills when she describes how she put together a presentation within a tight time frame. She also highlights her presentation skills.

Q. How have you convinced your boss that your approach is the best one to take in order to complete a project?

A. Before I started working for my current employer, employees rarely worked in teams. I knew many projects could best be worked on by a team rather than by an individual, but I couldn't seem to convince anyone else. Then my boss's supervisor asked her to work on a huge project with a very tight deadline. Even though my supervisor is a talented woman, this project clearly needed the talents of many different people to be successful. But I had to make her see that. I put together a list of people in different departments who, based on what I knew about them, had the necessary skills to help complete the project. I presented this list to my boss and sold her on the idea of putting together a team. She and her new team completed the project and her boss was extremely happy with it. My supervisor often uses teams to complete projects now.

This job candidate demonstrates how he is able to persuade his boss that his approach is the best one to take.

 ESSENTIAL

When choosing which accomplishment to discuss on a job interview, you should always select those accomplishments that best demonstrate your ability to do the job you are interviewing for.

Q. Explain what you do when you have a conflict with a client.

A. Last March I was working on a client's project that required us to hire a researcher. We worked closely with the client to draw up a contract with the researcher, who then completed the work. The client then decided he wanted some additional research done, but didn't want to pay for it. Of course, our researcher couldn't work for free, so we worked out a deal with her. We "loaned" her one of our interns to assist her, and she was able to charge less for the work she did. The client was happy that he got what he wanted and didn't have to pay full price for it. We were happy because he was pleased with our work, which meant that he would probably return in the future.

This interviewee shows how he resolves a conflict with a client by coming up with a solution everyone was happy with.

Q. Please tell me about a time you had to fire someone.

A. One of my employees suddenly started coming into work late every day. When it first started happening, I called him into my office to find out what was going on. I thought he might have some personal problem that was keeping him from getting to work on time. He assured me that he would make sure to get there punctually. The lateness stopped, and then started again a month later. I called him to my office again and reminded him that tardiness was unacceptable. Our company was big on flex-time, so I offered him a later schedule. He turned it down, saying that he couldn't work any later in the evening. Again he started arriving on time, but this time it only lasted two weeks. I had to let him go at that point. I explained the situation to him and he didn't seem very surprised.

This answer highlights the candidate's managerial skills.

CHAPTER 14

Do You Have Any Questions?

THE BULK OF THE JOB INTERVIEW will revolve around you. The interviewer will spend the entire length of it asking you questions that will help him learn as much as he can about you and how you fit into the company. Finally, as the interview is near its end, you will be given a chance to ask questions of your own. It is imperative that you are ready for that opportunity when it comes.

Why You Should Ask Questions

Of course, the obvious reason you should ask the interviewer questions is to get information that will guide you in your decision to accept or reject a job offer. So, with that in mind, if you think you have all the information you need to make a decision, should you say "no" when the interviewer asks you if you have any questions? Absolutely not!

While it is true that one of the reasons for asking questions at the end of the job interview is to help you make a decision about working for the employer, there are more reasons for doing so. Your questions will show the interviewer that you are interested in the job. The fact that you take time to ask questions will also show her that you are a careful decision-maker who needs to gather information before making a decision that is as serious as accepting a job offer.

Your questions also show that you were paying attention during the interview. To show that you really were paying attention, avoid asking questions that were already answered at some point during the interview. However, you can ask for clarification if you need it.

 ESSENTIAL

> During the interview, make mental notes of questions you want to ask based on questions the interviewer asks you. You may want clarification of something he says or you may simply want to show you were listening. Preface those questions with "You mentioned that . . ." or "Your question about . . . indicates that . . ."

Your questions give the interviewer a chance to picture you in the job. When possible, phrase your questions in a way that lets him do that. Instead of asking "What role will the person you hire play in the company's plans for expansion" ask "What role will I play in the company's expansion." This not only demonstrates your interest in the job, it also encourages the interviewer to consider your qualifications for the job and how they fit into the company's plans.

When you were preparing for the interview, you should have done some research to help you learn about the employer. Asking the interviewer to elaborate on information you learned from your research will prove that you did your homework. This signals to the employer that you are a motivated individual, which is desirable for a future employee.

Preparing Your Questions

You should prepare several questions before the job interview. Think of what information will help you decide whether you want to work for this employer. You will want to know about the company's future plans for growth, its current financial health, rates of employee turnover, levels of job satisfaction among employees, and what your chances for advancement are.

You may very likely come up with more questions during the interview. As mentioned previously, don't be afraid to ask for clarification of anything you didn't understand. Questions about salary, benefits, and vacation time are off limits at this point—hold on to those until an official job offer has been made.

 ALERT!

When you are asked if you have any questions, you should always have some prepared. If you don't ask any questions, the interviewer will assume either that you are not interested or that you make uninformed decisions. Neither will reflect well on you.

Q. Why is this job open?

This information will help you understand how you will be received should a job offer be made to you and should you accept it. If the person you will be replacing has left under difficult circumstances, that is, if he was fired or was otherwise forced to leave, his former coworkers may be resentful of anyone who fills his place. If the previous employee was promoted within the company, you taking the job may give you a chance for similar advancement down the line.

Q. Where is the job located?

This question, of course, is a practical one. Pity the person who accepts a job offer only to find out she has to relocate. From your research you will have learned whether the employer has offices elsewhere. The job advertisement will generally indicate which office has the job opening; if not, this is a fine question to ask.

Q. Is there a written job description? May I see it?

You will ask this question simply because you need this information to make an informed decision about whether or not to accept the job.

 ALERT!

Ideally, you should have information about the location and description of a job before the interview, but it may not have been readily available. Be careful, though. If the information was easy to access and you didn't manage to do it, you will look foolish if you ask for it at this late date.

Q. How long have you worked here?

The person interviewing you is in a job that is probably several steps above the one that you are interviewing for. Given that fact, the answer to this question will indicate how employees typically advance within the company. If the owner of the company is interviewing you, there is no reason to ask this question.

Q. What do you like most about your job with this company?

The interviewer is likely one of the few employees of the company with whom you will have contact before making your decision. See what she has to say about working there. The answer to this question, if the interviewer is honest, will weigh in to your decision about accepting a job offer. As with the previous question, ask this only of employees and not the owner of the company.

Q. What is the chain of command?

Whenever you ask questions about the inner workings of the company, it indicates to the employer that you are interested in the job.

Q. Who will I be reporting to?

If you find out who your immediate supervisor is, you can try to learn about that person. Don't forget that you should be gathering information that will help you decide whether to accept an offer if one is made.

Q. What does one need to do to advance?

Asking this question shows that you will be a productive employee who is interested in doing the best job possible. You will do what you need to do to move up.

Q. What are the chances for advancement?

Similar in nature to the previous question, this question shows the employer that you are motivated. It also allows you to find out if you will have the opportunity to advance should you work for that employer. That information will help you decide whether to accept a job offer, since you don't want to languish in the same position for a long time.

 ESSENTIAL

Take what you learn from the interviewer's answers and use that information to reiterate why you are the best candidate for the job. A thank-you letter, which you should send as a follow-up to the interview, is a good place to do this.

Q. How many people have held this position in the last three years? Why did they leave?

If there is a high rate of turnover in the position you are interviewing for, you should be suspicious. You should try to find out why this is the case. Is this a difficult employer to work for? Or perhaps the company has expectations that are impossible for employees to meet and they are fired for not meeting them. If you haven't already, access your network to find out if anyone has had any experience with this employer.

Q. How long do most employees stay?

Learning about turnover is a good way to gauge whether employees enjoy working for the employer. A high rate of turnover indicates that most employees aren't satisfied with their jobs, while a low rate of turnover demonstrates a high level of job satisfaction.

Q. What reason do most employees give for leaving?

The answer to this question expands on the answer to the prior question. Knowing why employees leave the company helps you find out what you may or may not like about working there. Of course, the interviewer may not know the answer to this question or may not be willing to share it.

 ALERT!

If the interviewer avoids answering questions about employee turnover or why employees leave the company, it should send up some red flags for you. You should try to find out, perhaps through your network, why people leave this company.

Q. How will you decide who to hire?

The answer to this question will let you find out if you missed something during the interview. Was there another skill or qualification the employer is seeking that you didn't get to talk about? By the time you get to ask this question, the interview will be drawing to a close. However, you can still follow up by sending a thank-you letter that will highlight the particular qualifications that you have and the employer is seeking.

Q. When will you make a decision?

If you know when the employer will make a hiring decision, you won't be left in a state of limbo waiting for the phone to ring. You can call the employer yourself—but it's best to wait one day after the employer says the decision is going to be made. If you are continuing to interview for other jobs, which you should do until you receive and accept a job offer, you might decide to schedule future interviews after that date, if it is close.

Q. How often are performance evaluations conducted and how are the evaluations made?

You will ask this question to learn what working for this company will be like. You may get a sense of how strict the managers are or how closely the staff is monitored. If you are interviewing for a management position, you will get a sense of how much of your time you will spend on evaluation paperwork.

Q. You mentioned something about a training period. How long is it?

This question indicates your interest in the job and shows that you were listening during the interview. It allows you to get clarification.

Q. Are there any other opportunities for training?

An employee who inquires about training opportunities is willing to learn as much as possible to do a good job.

Q. What types of assignments will I have?

This question indicates that you are interested in the job. It also allows you to learn what you will be doing if you are hired.

ALERT!

Phrase the question as if you are going to be hired. Not only will it show you are confident, it will let the employer picture you doing the assignments as she discusses them.

Q. How has the company grown over the last five years? Is it profitable?

A company's financial health will help you decide whether to accept a job offer. If the company hasn't grown over the last five years or if it isn't profitable, this should signal that it might not be in the best financial health. Should you accept a job offer, you may be looking for work again soon.

Q. What does the company plan to do to keep growing and what role would I play?

The answer to this question will give you information about your prospective employer and the job. You will learn what expectations the employer has for you. By phrasing the question like this, you give the interviewer the chance to picture you in the job he is interviewing you for.

Q. What improvements do you want to make here and how can I help you make them?

You will phrase this question the same way you phrased the previous one, allowing the employer to envision you as the person he will hire. It will give you a glimpse into the job and the company's plans for the future.

Q. In your opinion, how does this company compare to its major competitors, like Activate, Pump, and Dragon Works?

In preparing for the interview you should have researched the prospective employer. When you ask this question, you are saying to the interviewer "Look at the research I've done. I know who your competitors are." The answer to this question will also help you learn more about the company.

Q. From my research I learned you sell your products both in the United States and Canada. Do you plan to expand into any other markets?

Again you are stating something you uncovered in your research. You are also trying to learn something further about the company.

 ESSENTIAL

If the employer indicates that the company plans to expand into another market and you have experience with that market or just with that type of expansion, you can highlight that in your thank-you letter or in subsequent interviews.

Q. I know you sell hair-care products. What are the demographics of your customers?

Your reason for asking this question is similar to your reason for asking the prior one. If you have experience with the demographic this company targets, that is something you can talk about in your thank-you letter or in any follow-up interviews.

Q. You mentioned that several of your clients are in the apparel business. What industries are your other clients in?

This question shows you were paying attention during the interview. You also want to learn more about the company's other clients, which demonstrates your interest in the company.

Never Ask: How much money will I make?

Money should never be discussed on a job interview. You should hold off on discussing salary until you receive a job offer, when you will be able to negotiate. Even if the employer brings it up first, it is best to avoid getting into an extensive conversation about it at this point.

Never Ask: What are the health benefits like?

While you may need this information to help you decide whether or not to accept a job offer, the interview isn't the time to obtain it. Hold off on this discussion until you receive a job offer. The person interviewing you may not even know a lot about company benefits other than those he has.

Never Ask: How much vacation time will I have?

You haven't even started working and already you want to know about time off. Your goal during the interview is to demonstrate to the employer that you will be a productive employee. Asking about vacation time will not help you reach that goal.

Never Ask: Can I take time off for religious observance?

An employer is required by law to give you time off for religious observance, so you have no reason to ask about it during the interview. It should never be brought up in the interview or usually anytime before you begin working.

Never Ask: What does it take to get fired?

Asking this question is kind of like saying, "I want to do as little as possible to get by." Is that how you want the employer to see you?

 FACT

Questions about religion are off limits during a job interview. An employer cannot make a decision about whether or not to hire you based on your religion. The earliest you should bring it up or ask for religious observance time is after you've accepted a job offer.

CHAPTER 15

What to Do after the Interview

YOU SPENT DAYS, MAYBE EVEN WEEKS, getting ready for your job interview. You studied question after question, figuring out how you could best answer each one. You went through your work history to come up with anecdotes that would exemplify your ability to do the job you were being interviewed for. Now the interview is finally over and you think you should feel relieved, but you don't. You haven't been offered the job yet, so all you can do is sit around and wait. Right? Wrong!

Thank-You Letters

The first thing you should do after an interview, after sending the interviewer anything he requested, is send a thank-you letter. Job searchers sometimes feel that sending a thank-you letter will make them seem like they are trying to "kiss up" to the interviewer. You don't have any reason to think that, because interviewers rarely see it that way. Sending a thank-you letter is a nice gesture that will let the interviewer know you appreciate the time he spent meeting with you. It will set you apart from other job candidates who choose not to send one.

Who Should Get a Thank-You Letter?

You should send a thank-you letter to each person you met with during your interview. If you met with someone from the human resources department for a screening interview and then met with a department manager, each of them should receive a thank-you note. If someone showed you around the office, you should send that person a thank-you letter as well. If you had a panel or committee interview, you have to send a thank-you letter to each person who took part.

 ALERT!

Don't send letters addressed as "To Whom it May Concern." You should find out the name of each person who interviewed you. If possible, write it down or get that person's business card during the interview. If you didn't get a name, call the receptionist for that information. Make sure you get them all right—spelling counts.

What to Include

The primary purpose of a thank-you letter is to express your gratitude for the time the recipient spent with you. The first thing you should do is say "thank you." Next, take the opportunity to re-emphasize a skill or strength that shows you are the most qualified candidate for the job. If during the interview you neglected to mention a particular strength that might help the interviewer make her decision, bring that up in your thank-you letter. If the interviewer voiced concern about something regarding your qualifications, this would be a good time to address that issue.

 ESSENTIAL

Your letter should be short and to the point and should never be more than one page long. It should be written using a computer or typewriter, not handwritten. Never address the recipient by first name. Proofread your letter carefully and have someone else look it over too.

Finally, you should express your interest in the job. Tell the interviewer you want to work for her. Let her know how she can reach you even if you have already done so previously. Provide your phone number and an e-mail address if you have one. You want to make it as easy as possible for her to get in touch with you.

E-mail or Regular Mail?

You may wonder whether to send your thank-you letter by e-mail or regular mail, also known as snail mail. The problem with e-mail is that some people don't check theirs on a regular basis. It's hard for some of us to imagine that this is the case, but believe it or not, it is. If you've previously corresponded with the employer via e-mail, then it is perfectly okay to send a thank-you e-mail. If you haven't corresponded with her by e-mail up to that point, and have never been instructed to do so, then send your letter by regular mail. (See the following section for special formatting considerations for an e-mail thank-you note.)

How to Format a Thank-You Letter

A thank-you letter should be considered business correspondence and you must format it accordingly. In this age of electronic communication, many people have forgotten what a business letter even looks like. Here's the format you should use when writing a business letter. Skip a line after each of the following items:

- **Return address:** Your first and last name (no title) followed by your address should be the first thing on the page.
- **Date:** The date you are sending the letter should appear below the return address, with the name of the month spelled out.
- **Inside address:** The addressee's first and last name (including title, e.g., Mr., Ms., or Dr.), position, company name, and address should appear below the date. Start a new line for each of the following items: name, position, company, street address, and city/town/zip.

- **Salutation:** Your salutation should begin with "Dear" and you should always address the recipient by his or her title and last name, e.g., Mr. Grey, followed by a colon.
- **Body of letter:** The body of your letter should generally include an introductory paragraph that informs the reader why you are writing to him, one or two paragraphs to give some background or supporting information, and a closing paragraph that wraps everything up and includes information about how the interviewer can reach you.
- **Closing:** End your letter with "Yours truly" or "Sincerely."
- **Signature line:** Skip four or five lines after the closing for your signature, and then type your full name. (Don't forget to sign your letter above the typed signature line.)

Here are four sample thank-you letters. The first three are written to the actual interviewer and the final one is written to an administrative assistant who showed the candidate around the office. This letter is significantly shorter than the others, and does not make a point of reiterating any of the writer's skills, since its recipient will not be making the hiring decision and never discussed those skills with the candidate.

SAMPLE THANK-YOU LETTER #1

Joseph R. Green
14 Willow Street
Hoboken, NJ 07030

June 5, 2004

Ms. Maria Sanchez
Production Manager
Artistic Media
515 Madison Avenue
New York, NY 10022

Dear Ms. Sanchez:

Thank you for meeting with me this afternoon regarding the assistant production manager position at Artistic Media. I appreciate the time you spent getting to know me and explaining the specifics of the job.

I feel strongly that my experience and skills will allow me to make significant contributions to the production team. Artistic Media seems to be a company that values creativity, which is definitely one of my strengths.

I am looking forward to hearing from you within the week, as we discussed. Thank you again for your time and for considering me for this position. You can reach me by phone at (212) 555-4444 or by e-mail at *jgreene@rcat.net.*

Yours truly,

Joe Green

SAMPLE THANK-YOU LETTER #2

Beverly Smith
1524 South Jefferson Street
Williams, AZ 86046

September 21, 2004

Mr. Connor Shmedley
Customer Service Manager
Smart Mart Stores, Inc.
250 Adams Avenue
Flagstaff, AZ 86001

Dear Mr. Shmedley:

I appreciate your meeting with me this morning regarding the assistant customer service manager job at Smart Mart Stores. I enjoyed having the opportunity to talk to you about the improvements you have planned for the customer service department.

As I mentioned to you during the interview, before I moved to Williams, I worked at Bullseye Stores, which, as you know, has a great reputation for providing customer service. I worked closely with the department manager in implementing many of the procedures that earned Bullseye that reputation. I hope to have the opportunity to work with you to implement such procedures at Smart Mart.

Once again, thank you for taking time out of your busy schedule today. If you have any further questions, you can reach me by phone at (520) 555-5151 or by e-mail at *bevsmith@netco.com*. I look forward to hearing your decision soon.

Sincerely,

Beverly Smith

SAMPLE THANK-YOU LETTER #3

Sandy Beane
37 Oak Drive
Portland, OR 97205

June 24, 2004

Dr. Pat Lee
26 Tulip Street
Portland, OR 97201

Dear Dr. Lee:

Thank you for taking time out of your busy schedule this afternoon to interview me for the office manager position. I would welcome the opportunity to work with you and the members of your staff.

As you expressed in your interview, you are looking for someone who can manage a very busy office while showing compassion for your patients. As we discussed during the interview, though I did not work in a medical office, my experience managing a law office has provided me with the skills necessary to do this job well.

Again, thank you for meeting with me. If you have additional questions, you can reach me by phone at (503) 555-1234 or by e-mail at *sbeane@horizon.net*. I look forward to hearing from you regarding your decision.

Yours truly,

Sandy Beane

Rose Thornton
105 Peyton Place
Chicago, IL 60637

April 19, 2004

Mr. Richard Rheinhardt
Executive Assistant
Turning Corporation
1543 48th Street
Chicago, IL 60637

Dear Mr. Rheinhardt:

I just wanted to send a quick note to thank you for showing me around your offices on Tuesday after my interview with Janet Parker.

As Ms. Parker mentioned to you, I am interviewing for the bookkeeper position. Perhaps we will get to work together.

Yours truly,

Rose Thornton

Saying Thanks via E-mail

If you are going to send your thank-you letter by e-mail, you will use a different format than if you were sending it by postal mail. You will not place your return address at the top of the message. Instead you can include this below your name in the "signature" section of the message. You also don't need to include the recipient's address or the date.

Although the formatting is slightly different, sending a thank-you letter by e-mail does not give you an excuse to be any less formal than you would be if sending it by regular mail. In the salutation you will address the recipient by title and last name, never by first name. You will word your letter the same way you would have if you sent it by snail mail.

 ALERT!

> Do not use emoticons (a.k.a. smilies) or e-mail shorthand in your thank-you note. They will make you look unprofessional. Save those things for e-mail you send to your friends. The body of the note should follow the same guidelines as a note sent by regular mail.

If you are sending your thank-you letter by e-mail, use your personal e-mail account, not a work e-mail address. Do not send the e-mail from anyone's account but your own. If you share an e-mail account with your spouse, you might consider setting up your own account for professional use. Use a professional sounding e-mail address, preferably one that includes your name or initials.

What to Do If You Don't Want the Job

After the job interview you may decide that even if you receive a job offer you would not consider it. In that case you should take yourself out of the running early. While it may be tempting to wait to find out if you got the job, it would not be proper or considerate to do so.

Once you have decided you don't want the job after all, you should still send a thank-you letter. In that letter, you should thank the recipient for the time she spent meeting with you. You should explain that you no longer want to be considered for the job. If you would like to explain your reasons, go ahead. This is particularly important if you would like to be considered for some other position with the company in the future.

 ALERT!

If you decide you don't want the job on the day of the interview, wait twenty-four hours before you reveal this information to the employer. Give yourself time to change your mind. Once you send that letter, you can't take back your decision.

Here are two samples of thank-you letters that let an interviewer know you are no longer interested in the position.

THANK YOU, BUT I'M NO LONGER INTERESTED: SAMPLE LETTER #1

Lisa Evans
4141 Park Road
Evanston, IL 60201

October 3, 2004

Mr. David Grand
Senior Account Executive
Triangle Corporation
314 E. Pine Street
Evanston, IL 60201

Dear Mr. Grand:

Thank you for interviewing me yesterday for the position of assistant account executive. I appreciate the time you spent with me.

After careful consideration I have decided that I am no longer interested in this position.

Again, thank you for your time.

Yours truly,

Lisa Evans

THANK YOU, BUT I'M NO LONGER INTERESTED: SAMPLE LETTER #2

Thomas Jones
75 Bryant Avenue
San Francisco, CA 94108

August 6, 2004

Mr. Eric Peters
Vice President of Product Development
Q & H Corporation
402 West 3rd Street
San Francisco, CA 94108

Dear Mr. Peters:

Thank you for meeting with me yesterday afternoon regarding the marketing assistant position.

After mulling it over for the last twenty-four hours, I would like to take myself out of the running for this position. After spending three years in a similar job, I feel I am now ready for a greater challenge. If a position comes up in which I can better utilize my experience and skills, I hope you'll consider me.

Thank you again for your time. If you have any questions, please call me at (415) 555-2288 or e-mail me at *tjones@homenet.com.*

Sincerely,

Tom Jones

Waiting for a Decision

After the interview, you went home and sent thank-you letters to each person you met with. Now you are sitting around waiting for the phone to ring and checking your e-mail every five minutes. Is there anything else you can do to keep yourself from going crazy while you wait to hear something?

What to Do While You Wait

The best thing you can do while waiting to hear from a prospective employer is to stick to your usual routine. Doing so will help keep you sane as well as productive. If you are currently employed, your boss probably has no idea you are job hunting. Keep quiet about it even if you are pretty sure you will be offered the job you interviewed for. Nothing is ever a sure thing until you have an offer in writing. You should also keep your job search campaign active until you receive and accept an offer.

Following Up With the Employer

While there are many situations in your life where it's okay to play hard to get, your job search isn't one of them. There are many reasons you should contact the employer to find out if he has made a decision. There are no reasons not to make the call.

Following up on a job interview is not only your right, it is an important strategy that should be part of your job search campaign. A phone call to a prospective employer shows that you are not someone who is willing to sit around and wait quietly while someone else makes a decision about your future. It also gives you another opportunity to sell yourself to the employer if you find out she hasn't yet made a decision.

You may be hesitant to call an employer to find out if she has made a hiring decision because you don't want to look anxious or pushy. As long as you go about it in the right way, you won't. You should call the employer exactly one week after the interview, unless the interviewer told you she would be making a decision by a certain date. In that case, call a day after that date.

ALERT!

Don't make a pest of yourself by calling your prospective employer too often. If the employer tells you he will make a decision in a week, don't call back before then. As a general rule, don't call more than once a week. You don't want the act of finding out whether you got the job to cost you the job.

Call the person who has been your contact at the prospective employer's company. Politely, but not meekly, ask if they have made a decision yet. If they haven't, ask when they expect to make one.

The Job Offer—Finally

So, you have a job offer. Congratulations! By this time it's likely that you've decided whether you want to work for the company. Of course, you will have to consider the offer they made and decide whether to accept it. You may have to negotiate for a better offer if you find that the one they made wasn't satisfactory.

If you decide to negotiate for a better offer, be sure to do your homework first. You should know what the typical salaries are for those with your experience in your field. You should also be aware of regional salary differences; if your best friend is working in the big city and the job you are being offered is in the suburbs, the salary may be less. If you get extensive benefits, such as health insurance, your salary may be lower.

Before you do anything, ask the employer to send you the offer in writing. Do not give notice to your current employer until you have something in writing from your future employer. You should, in turn, accept the job offer in writing. If you decide to decline, do that in writing as well. Good luck with your new job!

Resources

Career-Related Web Sites

6FigureJobs

☞ *www.6figurejobs.com*

Executives can post their resumes and search for jobs for free on this Web site.

About Career Planning

☞ *http://careerplanning.about.com*

The Everything® Practice Interview Book author Dawn Rosenberg McKay's site covers all aspects of career planning including career choice, job hunting, job training, legal issues, and the workplace.

About Job Searching

☞ *http://jobsearch.about.com*

Alison Doyle, the guide to this excellent site, helps you with all aspects of online job searching, writing resumes and cover letters, references, interviewing skills, and unemployment.

About Job Searching: Technical

☞ *http://jobsearchtech.about.com*

Guide J. Steven Niznik keeps you updated on the technical job market. Get the latest information on health care, engineering, semi-conducter, science, Internet, and telecom jobs.

Action Words from Missouri Works!

✑ *www.works.state.mo.us/ultimate/section3/actionwords.htm*

You can use the action words listed on this site to describe your skills and knowledge.

CareerMag.com

✑ *www.careermag.com*

At this site, you can search for jobs by career, industry, keyword, or location.

CareerBuilder.com

✑ *www.careerbuilder.com*

Through its partnerships with newspaper publishers Tribune, Gannett, and Knight Ridder, *CareerBuilder.com* lists local jobs from newspaper help wanted sections from around the country. Search this huge jobs database by location, company, job type, and industry. You can even search in Spanish.

Career Journal

✑ *www.careerjournal.com*

Career Journal is the *Wall Street Journal*'s executive career site and is geared toward executives, managers, and professionals. It includes salary and hiring information, job search advice, and career management help. There is also a searchable database of jobs in select fields.

CollegeGrad.com

✑ *www.collegegrad.com*

This job board targets college graduates and recent graduates. In addition to job listings you'll find information on career choice, job search advice, and salary information.

Company Research from About Career Planning

✑ *http://careerplanning.about.com/cs/companyresearch*

Find out what resources you can use to do company research. Learn how to access business directories and news sources.

The Equal Employment Opportunity Commission
✍ *www.eeoc.gov*

Use this Web site to learn more about the laws that protect workers from discrimination at work.

ExecutivePlanet.com
✍ *www.executiveplanet.com*

This Web site includes business culture guides for international businesspeople.

FlipDog.com
✍ *www.flipdog.com*

FlipDog.com collects job announcements from company Web sites. Search for jobs by employer, keyword, and category. Post your resume.

JobHuntersBible.com
✍ *www.jobhuntersbible.com*

Dick Bolles, the author of *What Color Is Your Parachute?* runs this site as a supplement to his well-known book. He has included a variety of tools, including career and personality tests and advice that will help you with your career and job search.

JobStar Profession-Specific Salary Surveys
✍ *www.jobstar.org/tools/salary/sal-prof.cfm*

Get salary information for dozens of professions.

Monster
✍ *www.monster.com*

Search for jobs by location or job category. You can also enter key words to search by job titles, company names, and requirements. Post your resume online so employers can find you.

Monster Career Advice
✍ *http://content.monster.com*

Resume and job interviewing tips, salary information, relocating advice, and diversity advice from Monster.com.

NewsLink

✑ *http://newslink.org*

This site provides links to business journals around the country.

Occupational Outlook Handbook

✑ *www.bls.gov/oco/home.htm*

Use this resource, published by the U.S. Bureau of Labor Statistics, to find out what workers do on the job. Learn about working conditions, training and education needed, employment outlook, salary, and expected job prospects for a wide number of occupations.

Public Service Employees Network

✑ *www.pse-net.com*

You'll find links to local government job listings on this site.

Quintessential Careers

✑ *www.quintcareers.com*

Get job search and career advice. You'll find links to job banks, career advice for teens and college grads, and tutorials to help you with job interviews and writing a resume and cover letter.

Riley Guide

✑ *www.rileyguide.com*

Librarian Margaret F. Dikel has organized myriad sites that can help you with your job search.

Salary.com

✑ *www.salary.com*

Get salary information for a variety of occupations.

SEC Filings and Forms (EDGAR)

✑ *www.sec.gov/edgar.shtml*

The Securities and Exchange Commission requires publicly held companies to file information about finances quarterly and information about material events or corporate changes as they occur. You can retrieve this information from the EDGAR database.

USAJOBS

✍ *www.usajobs.opm.gov*

This is the official Web site of the U.S. Federal Government. Job listings for all federal jobs are posted here. Post and store a resume that you can use to apply for jobs on this site.

Vault

✍ *www.vault.com*

When you're preparing for a job interview, Vault is the place to go. You'll find company and industry profiles. There are message boards where employees share information about their employers. There's also a free job board that lists thousands of openings.

Yahoo! HotJobs

✍ *www.hotjobs.com*

Search for a job by keyword, job category, or location. Post your resume and let employers find you. You can cut and paste your current resume or use Resume Builder to get help creating a new one.

Books

Job Search

The Back Door Guide to Short-Term Job Adventures, by Michael Landes. CA: Ten Speed Press, 2002.

Cyberspace Job Search Kit: The Complete Guide to Online Job Seeking and Career Information, by Mary B. Nemnich and Fred E. Jandt. IN: JIST Works, 2001.

Federal Civil Service Jobs, by Dawn Rosenberg McKay and Michele Lipson. NJ: Peterson's, 2002.

JobBank Series, Adams Media, Annual.

Job-Hunting for the So-Called Handicapped or People Who Have Disabilities, by Richard Nelson Bolles and Dale S. Brown. IN: JIST Works, 2001.

Cover Letters and Resumes

101 Best Cover Letters, by Jay A. Block and Michael Betrus. NY: McGraw-Hill, 1999.

101 Grade A Resumes for Teachers, by Rebecca Anthony and Gerald Roe. NY: Barron's Educational Series, 2003.

201 Killer Cover Letters, by Sandra Podesta and Andrea Paxton. NY: McGraw-Hill, 2003.

Ace the IT Resume!, by Paula Moreira and Robyn Thorpe. CA: Osborne/McGraw-Hill, 2002.

Adams Cover Letter Almanac, Adams Media, MA, 1995.

Adams Resume Almanac, Adams Media, MA, 1994.

America's Top Resumes for America's Top Jobs, by Michael Farr. IN: JIST Works, 2002.

Best Resumes for $100,000+ Jobs, by Wendy S. Enelow. VA: Impact Publications, 1997.

Best Resumes for College Students and New Grads, by Louise M. Kursmark. IN: JIST Works, 2003.

Blue Collar Resumes, by Steven Provenzano. NJ: Career Press, 1999.

Cover Letters that Knock 'em Dead, by Martin Yate. MA: Adams Media, 2004.

The Damn Good Resume Guide: A Crash Course in Resume Writing, by Yana Parker. CA: Ten Speed Press, 2002.

Designing the Perfect Resume, by Pat Criscito. NY: Barron's Educational Series, 2000.

The Edge Resume and Job Search Strategy, by Bill Corbin and Shelbi Wright. IN: JIST Works, 2000.

The Everything® Cover Letter Book, by Steven Graber. MA: Adams Media, 2000.

The Everything® Resume Book, Second Edition, by Burton Jay Nadler. MA: Adams Media, 2003.

Expert Resumes for Computer and Web Jobs, by Wendy S. Enelow and Louise M. Kursmark. IN: JIST Works, 2002.

Expert Resumes for Health Care Careers, by Wendy S. Enelow and Louise M Kursmark. IN: JIST Works, 2004.

Expert Resumes for People Returning to Work, by Wendy S. Enelow and Louise M. Kursmark. IN: JIST Works, 2003.

Gallery of Best Resumes, by David F. Noble. IN: JIST Works, 2001.

Gallery of Best Resumes for People Without a Four-Year Degree, by David F. Noble. IN: JIST Works, 2000.

The Insider's Guide to Writing the Perfect Resume by Karl Weber and Rob Kaplan. NJ: Peterson's, 2001.

Real Resumes for Financial Jobs, edited by Anne McKinney. Fayetteville, NC: Prep Publishing, 2001.

The Resume Catalog: 200 Damn Good Examples, by Yana Parker. CA: Ten Speed Press, 1996.

Resume Magic, by Susan Britton Whitcomb. IN: JIST Works, 2003.

Resumes That Get Jobs, 10th ed., edited by Ray Potter. NJ: Arco, 2002.

Resumes that Knock 'em Dead, by Martin Yate. MA: Adams Media, 2002.

Sales and Marketing Resumes for $100,000 Careers, by Louise Kursmark. IN: JIST Works, 2000.

Top Secret Executive Resumes: What It Takes to Create the Perfect Resume for the Best Top-Level Positions, by Steven Provenzano. NJ: Career Press, 2000.

Vault Guide to Resumes, Cover Letters and Interviewing 2002 Edition, by the editors of Vault. NY: Vault, 2001.

Interview Etiquette and Style

Adams Job Interview Almanac, Adams Media, MA, 1996.

Business Etiquette: 101 Ways to Conduct Business with Charm and Savvy, by Ann Marie Sabath. NJ: Career Press, 2002.

Chic Simple Dress Smart for Men: Wardrobes That Win in the Workplace, by Kim Johnson Gross and Jeff Stone. NY: Warner Books, 2002.

Chic Simple Dress Smart for Women: Wardrobes That Win in the Workplace, by Kim Johnson Gross and Jeff Stone. NY: Warner Books, 2002.

Emily Post's the Etiquette Advantage in Business, by Emily Post and Peter Post. NY: HarperCollins, 1999.

Esquire's Things a Man Should Know About Handshakes, White Lies, and Which Fork Goes Where, by Ted Allen and Scott Omelianuk. New York: Hearst Communications, 2001.

Gestures: The Do's and Taboos of Body Language Around the World, by Roger E. Axtell and Mike Fornwald. NY: John Wiley & Sons, 1997.

Your Executive Image: How to Look Your Best and Project Success for Men and Women, by Victoria A. Seitz. MA: Adams Media Corporation, 2000.

International Job Searching

Best Resumes and CVs for International Jobs: Your Passport to the Global Job Market, by Ronald L. Krannich and Wendy S. Enelow. VA: Impact Publications, 2002.

Dun and Bradstreet's Guide to Doing Business Around the World, by Terri Morrison, Wayne A. Conaway, and Joseph J. Douress. NJ: Prentice Hall Press, 2000.

Global Etiquette Guide to Europe: Everything You Need to Know for Business and Travel Success, by Dean Allen Foster. NY: John Wiley & Sons, 2000.

International Jobs: Where They Are and How to Get Them, by Nina Segal and Eric Kocher. NY: Perseus Publishing, 2003.

General

The 7 Habits of Highly Effective People, by Stephen R. Covey. NY: Free Press, 1989.

Building Your Career Portfolio, by Carol A. Poore. NJ: Career Press, 2001.

Communicate with Confidence, by Dianna Booher. NY: McGraw-Hill, 1994.

The Everything® Get-A-Job Book, by Steven Graber. MA: Adams Media, 2000.

Get Paid What You're Worth: The Expert Negotiators' Guide to Salary and Compensation, by Robin L. Pinkley and Gregory B. Northcraft. NY: St. Martin's Press, 2003.

How to Say It at Work: Putting Yourself across with Power Words, Phrases, Body Language, and Communication Secrets, by Jack Griffin. NJ: Prentice Hall Press, 1998.

Kick off Your Career: Write a Winning Resume, Ace Your Interview, Negotiate a Great Salary, by Kate Wendleton. NJ: Career Press, 2002.

Make a Name for Yourself: 8 Steps Every Woman Needs to Create a Personal Brand Strategy for Success, by Robin Fisher Roffer. NY: Broadway Books, 2000.

Negotiating Your Salary: How to Make $1000 a Minute, by Jack Chapman. CA: Ten Speed Press, 2000.

The Networking Survival Guide: Get the Success You Want by Tapping into the People You Know, by Diane Darling. NY: McGraw-Hill, 2003.

Power Interviews: Job-Winning Tactics from Fortune 500 Recruiters, by Neil Yeager and Lee Hough. NY: John Wiley & Sons, 1998.

The Smart Woman's Guide to Resumes and Job Hunting, by Julie Adair King and Betsy Sheldon. NJ: Career Press, 1995.

SuperNetworking, by Michael Salmon. NJ: Career Press, 2003.

Targeting the Job You Want, by Kate Wendleton. NJ: Career Press, 2000.

What Color Is Your Parachute: A Practical Manual for Job-Hunters and Career-Changers, by Richard Nelson Bolles. CA: Ten Speed Press, 2003.

Women for Hire: The Ultimate Guide to Getting a Job, by Tory Johnson, Robyn Freedman Spizman, and Lindsey Pollak. NY: Berkley Publishing Group, 2002.

Glossary

acceptance letter: A letter informing an employer of one's decision to accept a job offer.

accomplishment: Something at which you succeeded as a direct result of your efforts.

achievement: See *accomplishment*.

Americans with Disabilities Act (ADA): A federal civil rights law that was designed to prevent discrimination and enable those with disabilities to participate fully in all aspects of society.

annual report: The primary document most public companies use to disclose corporate information to shareholders.

background check: Used by prospective employers to verify the information included on a job candidate's resume or application, including work history and educational background. May also include looking at criminal records and credit history.

behavioral interview: An interview during which the interviewer asks the job candidate to demonstrate her competencies by giving real-life examples of when she has used those competencies. This may be either a standalone entity or part of a regular job interview.

benefits: The part of your compensation package that is in addition to salary. May include health and life insurance, personal days, vacation, pension plans, tuition assistance, and severance packages.

body language: The nonverbal gestures and mannerisms used to interpret one's true feelings.

career exploration: This step of the career-planning process involves gathering information about an occupation in order to make a decision regarding career choice.

Certified Professional Resume Writer (CPRW): A resume writer who is certified by the Professional Association of Resume Writers.

chronological resume: A resume on which work experience is listed in reverse chronological order (that is, the most recent job is at the top of the list).

Civil Rights Act of 1964, Title VII: This federal law prohibits employment discrimination based on an individual's race, religion, sex, or national origin.

civil service: Employment in the federal government, or in a state or local government.

combination resume: A resume that combines the information included on both a functional and a chronological resume. Skills are emphasized but an employment history is included.

committee interview: See *panel interview*

competencies: A combination of your knowledge, skills, and abilities.

confidentiality agreement: Part of an employment contract that prohibits an employee from disclosing confidential or sensitive information. Also referred to as a *nondisclosure agreement*.

corporate culture: The shared values, goals, and practices that give a corporation its unique personality.

cover letter: A letter sent along with a resume. The cover letter's purpose is to introduce the job seeker to the person who will be reviewing the resume and to express the candidate's interest in the job.

curriculum vitae (CV): A summary of one's work experience that is much more detailed than a resume; includes academic background, publications, and other professional achievements.

Equal Employment Opportunity Commission (EEOC): The federal agency that oversees the enforcement of antidiscrimination laws.

exempt employee: Refers to employees who are exempt from the overtime and minimum wage provisions of the Fair Labor Standards Act. Exempt employees are generally those working in executive, administrative, professional, or outside sales positions.

Fair Labor Standards Act (FLSA): U.S. law that establishes minimum wage, overtime pay, record-keeping, and child labor standards. These standards affect nonexempt full-time and part-time employees in the private sector as well as in federal, state, and local governments.

Family and Medical Leave Act (FLMA): Enacted in 1993, this federal law allows for a leave from work for the birth or adoption of a child or one's own illness or that of a family member.

Form 10-Q: A quarterly report that a publicly held company files with the SEC.

Form 8-K: The form a publicly held company files with the SEC to report the occurrence of any material events or corporate changes.

functional resume: A resume on which skills are categorized by job function. Abilities are emphasized rather than work history.

glass ceiling: A term that refers to the invisible barrier which certain groups, e.g., women and minorities, cannot pass to reach higher career levels.

goal, long-term: A career or personal objective that can take from three to five years to complete.

goal, short-term: A career or personal objective that can be reached in one to three years.

group interview: A job interview during which a group of candidates are interviewed at the same time.

hard skills: The skills you learned in school or through some other formal training. See also *soft skills.*

hiring manager: The person for whom a job candidate will work if hired. The hiring manager interviews and selects the candidate.

human resources (HR) department: The department in a company that is responsible for selection, hiring, and training employees. Sometimes referred to as the *personnel department.*

illegal questions: Technically, the questions that a prospective employer cannot, by law, ask a job candidate. Often refers to questions used to gather information which the employer cannot use to make a hiring decision because of antidiscrimination laws. See also *Equal Employment Opportunity Commission.*

informational interview: A meeting during which someone planning his or her career learns about a field of work from someone who has firsthand knowledge.

internship: Term of practical experience in one's field of study under supervision. Interns are sometimes paid.

interpersonal skills: The skills one uses to get along with others.

job announcement: see *job posting*.

job banks: Web sites that list job openings and allow users to search through them by location, job type, and often keywords such as job title and employer. See also *resume banks*.

job club: A group of people who meet to offer support to one another during the job search process. Usually help is offered regarding resume writing, job interviewing, and networking.

job coach: See *career coach*.

job description: Provides details about a job, such as duties, requirements, and hours.

job objective: The section of the resume that tells a prospective employer what type of job the candidate is seeking.

job offer: An offer made to a job candidate by the prospective employer. The job offer usually includes specifics about the job, such as salary, benefits, hours, and starting date.

job posting: A notice announcing that a job is available. It usually gives some details about the position and its requirements.

job reference: Someone who the potential employer may contact to ask about a job candidate. Generally this person will be able to recommend that the employer hire this person.

job reference list: A neatly formatted list of job references that includes names and contact information.

mentor: One who provides guidance for a less-experienced colleague.

mock job interview: A practice job interview, possibly video-taped.

network: The group of individuals to whom one can turn for help.

noncompete agreement: Part of an employment contract or a separate agreement that states that one will not compete with his or her employer. An employee may be asked to sign a noncompete agreement upon being hired. Also referred to as a noncompete clause.

nondisclosure agreement: See *confidentiality agreement*.

nonexempt employee: Refers to employees who are covered by the Fair Labor Standards Act. Nonexempt employees must receive overtime pay and the current minimum wage.

panel interview: A job interview during which a group of people ask questions of the job candidate. Also referred to as a *committee interview.*

personality inventory: A tool used to find out what personality type one fits into. Personality inventories are used as self-assessment tools.

portfolio: A collection of work. A portfolio generally contains pictures, photographs, or writing samples but may include any work samples a job candidate wants a prospective employer to see.

pregnancy discrimination act: Amends Title VII of the Civil Rights Act of 1964 to protect a woman from being discriminated against based on her pregnancy or related condition.

privately held company: A company owned by individuals or groups of individuals.

publicly held company: A company with shareholders who have a financial stake in the company.

qualifications: The knowledge, skills, and abilities a job candidate must have in order to be hired for a particular position.

reasonable accommodation: Adjustments or modifications provided by an employer to enable people with disabilities to enjoy equal employment opportunities.

reference: See *job reference.*

rejection letter: A letter informing an employer of one's decision to reject a job offer.

resume: A short summary of one's work history and educational background. A resume is usually one page in length. See also *chronological resume, combination resume,* and *functional resume.*

resume banks: Web sites that allow users to post resumes so employers may search through them to find eligible applicants.

salary history: A document included as an addendum to the resume. Lists salaries for each job on the resume.

salary negotiation: The process a job candidate goes through to obtain the best possible compensation package.

selection interview: The interview during which the hiring manager will try to determine if the applicant is the best-qualified job candidate.

sexual harassment: Unwelcome sexual advances, requests for sexual favors, or other verbal or physical conduct of a sexual nature. Rejection of this conduct may have a negative effect on one's employment, work performance, or create an intimidating, hostile, or offensive work environment. Sexual harassment violates the Civil Rights Act of 1964.

screening interview: The initial interview with a prospective employer. Usually someone from the human resources department will try to verify items on the candidate's resume, such as dates of employment, schooling, etc.

Securities and Exchange Commission (SEC): The U.S. government agency that protects investors and maintains the integrity of the securities market.

soft skills: Skills that aren't specific to any occupation, but instead enhance one's performance regardless of what one's actual job is. See also *hard skills*.

stress interview: A technique sometimes used by interviewers to weed out job candidates who can't handle adversity. The interviewer purposely makes the candidate uncomfortable or anxious.

thank-you letter: A letter the job candidate sends, following a job interview, to each person who participated in the job interview.

transferable skills: Skills one has gathered through jobs, hobbies, volunteer work, or other life experiences that can be used in future jobs or in a new career.

work history: Past jobs as described on one's resume.

vita: See *curriculum vitae*.

Index

A

accomplishments
  preparing to discuss, 73–75
  sample questions and answers
    about, 76–90, 157, 242
advancement, questions about,
  249–251
Age Discrimination in Employment
  Act of 1967, 202, 204
age issues
  candidate's age, 196, 202, 204, 205
  supervisor's age, 193
  workforce statistics, 193
Americans with Disabilities Act of
  1990, 203, 204, 215–216
anecdotes, 6, 223
anxiety, 16–17, 29, 51, 55–57, 179
appearance, 18, 19–23
arrival, at interview, 24–27
assertiveness, 131

B

behavioral interview
  reasons for, 221–223
  sample questions and answers,
    224–243
body language, 14, 28–31, 36
boss
  disagreeing with, 131
  discussing previous, 114
  discussing unhappiness with job
    with, 144
  disliking of, 134–135
  predicting reactions of, 125
budgeting, 177, 236
Bureau of Labor Statistics, 149

C

caffeine, 18
career progress, 76–78, 122

casual dress, 20–21
certification, 171
challenges, 172
change, 47
character traits, *see* interpersonal
  skills
children, questions about, 210–211
choices, *see* decision-making
Civil Rights Act of 1964, Title VII,
  202, 203–204, 209
clothing
  for interview, 19–23
  for job, 169
college, *see* education
communication skills, 67. *See also*
  writing and presentation skills
company directories, 13
computer literacy, 62–63
confidence, 17, 170
confidentiality, 175
conflict resolution, 128–129, 232,
  243. *See also* supervisory skills
convictions (legal), 191, 214
cost-cutting, 177
courses
  in college, 96–98, 101–104
  plans for future, 104
co-worker, ideal, 137
crimes, 191, 214
crisis, handling of, 61, 88
criticism, 144
customer service, 142–143, 172

D

date, being asked on, 140
decision-making
  about career, 53
  at college, 93–94, 95, 102,
    107–108
  on the job, 50, 119–121, 179, 229,
    232, 240
  unpopular decisions and, 135
delegation, 61, 230, 239, 241

S

T

U

V

W

OTHER EVERYTHING® TITLES
YOU MIGHT ENJOY . . .

The Everything® Cover Letter Book, 2nd Edition
1-59337-335-X
$14.95 ($19.95 CAN)

The Everything® Job Interview Book
1-58062-493-6
$14.95 ($19.95 CAN)

The Everything® Resume Book, 2nd Edition
1-58062-807-9
$14.95 ($19.95 CAN)